Culture as Polyphony

. . . There's a hell of a good universe
next door; let's go.

—e.e. cummings

. . . A new scientific truth does not triumph by
convincing its opponents and making them see the
light, but rather because its opponents eventually
die, and a new generation grows up that is familiar
with it.

—Max Planck

Culture as Polyphony
An Essay on the Nature of Paradigms

James M. Curtis

University of Missouri Press
Columbia & London, 1978

Copyright © 1978 by The Curators of the University of Missouri
University of Missouri Press, Columbia, Missouri 65211
Library of Congress Catalog Card Number 77–25242
Printed and bound in the United States of America

Library of Congress Cataloging in Publication Data
Curtis, James M.,   1940–
    Culture as polyphony.

    Bibliography: p.
    Includes index.
    1.   Analogy.   2.   McLuhan, Herbert Marshall.
Understanding media.   3.   Communication.
4.   Communication and traffic.   5.   Technology and civilization.
6.   Civilization, Modern—20th century. I.   Title.
BD190.C8   169   77–25242
ISBN 0–8262–0251–9

Permissions on last page.

To three people from Tupelo:
My parents, Malcolm and Earsel Curtis,
and Elvis Presley, *in memoriam*

Preface

In the title and subtitle of this book I have used two problematic terms, *polyphony* and *paradigm*. Although these words have specific meanings in musicology and linguistics, respectively, I have used them in a new, more general, and metaphorical sense. It may therefore help to clarify the title by stating what *polyphony* and *paradigm* will mean in this book.

Polyphony and *polyphonic* do have technical meanings. They

are applied to "many-sound" or "many-voiced" music, i.e., to music in which instead of the parts marching in step with one another, and without particular interest in their individual melodic curves, they move in apparent independence and freedom though fitting together harmonically.[1]

Modernism, the innovative movement in the arts that dominated the first half of the twentieth century, developed a metaphorical sense of polyphony by taking from the musicological definition the concept of a dynamic structure that consists of interacting parts, and by using it to characterize, justify, or explain various innovations in the visual and verbal arts—not just in music. Although this metaphorical sense of polyphony first appeared in the late nineteenth century, historically the most important such uses of the term occur around 1930. Three creative men, the Swiss painter Paul Klee, the Russian critic Mikhail Bakhtin, and the Polish philosopher Roman Ingarden, all used it in various ways. Klee, for instance, gave his paintings titles like *Polyphonic White* (1929); Bakhtin used the term *polyphonic novel* in his brilliant, seminal *Problems of Dostoyevsky's Work* (1929); and Ingarden's *The Literary Work of Art* (1932) uses *polyphony* in developing his interpretation of a work of art as multileveled.

In this book I generalize these uses of polyphony, rather as Klee, Bakhtin, and Ingarden generalized the musicological definition, for I

1. Percy A. Scholes, *The Oxford Companion to Music,* 10th ed., John Owen Ward, ed. (London: Oxford University Press, 1970), p. 820.

will use the term to characterize the social processes of which culture consists. Whereas the modernists thought of a work of art as a dynamic process with parts that interact to create a heterogeneous whole, I wish to think of culture as a heterogeneous whole whose various aspects, such as art and cognition, interact polyphonically. (Claude Lévi-Strauss has used musical terms for analogous reasons in his *The Raw and the Cooked.*) With Jacques Derrida,[2] I believe that key terms, *especially* metaphorical terms, have epistemological implications and that the more consciously one uses such terms and metaphors, the more rigorous one's work becomes. My epistemological reasons for calling this book *Culture as Polyphony* will become apparent in Part I.

I use the other special term, *paradigm,* in a metaphorical way as well. If *polyphony* refers to music, *paradigm* refers to language, and in the linguistics of Ferdinand de Saussure and Roman Jakobson, *language* always means *spoken language.* Thus *polyphony* and *paradigm* both refer to sound, a fact that gives them a certain consonance.

In linguistics, *paradigm* refers to a pattern that recurs in particular groups of words and thus makes specific utterances meaningful, as in the sequence of endings in the Latin verb forms *amo, amas, amat.* But for several centuries this word, in English at least, has had a metaphorical meaning as well. The *Oxford English Dictionary* cites the following use from 1669: "The Universe . . . was made exactly conformable to its Paradigm, or universal Exemplar."[3]   While I do not believe in Neoplatonism and make no commitment to the seventeenth century's concept of a "universal Exemplar," I do believe that by generalizing *paradigm* to include all human behavior, not just speech, one acquires a very powerful concept. Lest misunderstanding arise on this issue, I emphasize that paradigms do not operate in a mechanical way. Paradigms do not create uniform, repeatable instances of *anything,* whether of language or of behavior. Paradoxical as it may seem, paradigms—in the general sense in which I will be using the term— make all forms of creativity possible.

2. Cf. Derrida's statement, "The general taxonomy of metaphors—of what are called philosophical metaphors in particular— . . . presupposes a solution to important problems, and first of all to problems which actually generate the whole of philosophy and its history." Jacques Derrida, "White Mythology: Metaphor in the Text of Philosophy," *New Literary History* 4:1 (Autumn 1974):28.

3. *The Oxford English Dictionary* (Oxford: Clarendon Press, 1933), 7:449.

Culture as Polyphony really had its origins in Tupelo, Mississippi, where I grew up, and where Elvis Presley also grew up. In a way, I wrote it to resolve the tensions that I came to feel between the culture of Tupelo and the culture of New York City, where I got a Ph.D. in Russian literature at Columbia University. In artistic terms, the tension stretches between Elvis Presley's "Don't Be Cruel," which evokes in me a memory of a particular afternoon in Tupelo, and Fyodor Dostoyevsky's *Crime and Punishment,* which I associate with a particularly intense revelation about the symbolic meaning of bridges. It seems to me that most people, if confronted with these two very different works, would probably express a preference for one or the other, at least aesthetically, and that this choice would imply much about the way they live. But I have found myself unable to choose between them. I have responded intensely to them both, and still do. For many years I could not explain or justify—even to myself—my inability to choose between them and all that they represent, and this book expresses my own need to use a paradigm that excludes neither songs like "Don't Be Cruel," nor novels like *Crime and Punishment.* I hope that in what I say here I can serve as a cultural mediator for others who feel similar tensions and contradictions.

My first intimation of this role of mediator came about with the kind of irony that others who have experienced considerable social mobility may appreciate. I decided to study Russian literature in graduate school, because I wanted to reject everything that small Southern towns represented. What better way, I thought, to do this than to study something exotic in the Big Apple itself? As an alienated adolescent in Tupelo, I had often dreamed of the sophisticated life that I would someday lead in the big city. Imagine my surprise when I discovered, not sophistication, but another kind of provincialism, a no less tenacious kind, in New York.

But something else was going on as well. In my classes at Columbia I often felt frustrated at what I considered the stupidity of the Russians' belief in the specialness and uniqueness of their country because it all sounded so familiar—it sounded like what Southerners have always said about the South. I began to realize that I perceived Russia, and Russians, differently from my fellow students and my teachers. The beauty and repulsiveness of Russian culture had a personal resonance for me—they always reminded me of the beauty and repulsiveness of Southern culture. That which I had sought to escape proved a great source of strength and meaning.

Stubbornly at first and then with increasing fascination and even pride, I began to sense the many similarities between the American South and Russia. Both have existed primarily as agrarian societies in which modernization has proceeded at a dizzying and often destructive pace. Both have responded to this change by trying to deny its existence and effects, and both have compensated for an obsessive sense of cultural inferiority by a fervent regionalism. Regionalism often gives rise to demagoguery, and both cultures have a history of violence and racism in which a decadent aristocracy has played a major role. Finally, much creativity has come from both, especially in the twentieth century, when cultural innocence and sophistication have had complex, changing relationships. At some time in the future I hope to make these general analogies more specific by studying the relationship between *War and Peace* and *Gone With the Wind*, and the similar roles of these novels as historical myths in Russia and the South, respectively.

In this book, however, I have more general aims, for I have long felt the need to treat general, theoretical problems first. Somehow it seemed to me that the task required a concept of the nature of culture, cultural change, and the role of art, and I couldn't find anybody in my student days who seemed to feel that these problems mattered very much.

Then came the memorable day when I started reading Marshall McLuhan's *Understanding Media*, and everything clicked. As I read McLuhan's nonlinear, nonexpository prose, I kept saying to myself, "Of course! Of course! That explains it." *Of course* the South and Russia resembled each other; in McLuhan's terms, they were both oral societies in which literacy had appeared relatively late and had increased relatively slowly. I had found a way of making the vital connections between specific facts in various cultures and the general principles of a unified system. To my delight, the system gave me a way of understanding both Elvis Presley and Fyodor Dostoyevsky. But as a line from one of Elvis's songs has it, that's when my troubles really began.

They began when I started talking to my acquaintances about the possibility of applying McLuhan's work to specific problems. I encountered indifference, if not downright hostility. My suggestion that a book on the bestseller list could have anything to do with Dostoyevsky struck them as bizarre, at the very least. I now perceive their reactions as typical results of the dichotomy between high culture and popular culture, between sophistication and simplicity.

At the time, though, this indifference and hostility puzzled me as much as Russian nationalism had earlier. It puzzled me until I found in Thomas B. Kuhn's *The Structure of Scientific Revolutions* the term and concept of *paradigm,* in the sense that I use it in this book. After reading Kuhn and applying his work to my own situation, it seemed clear to me that McLuhan called into question the validity of the paradigm that my acquaintances used. This meant that he, and anyone who used his paradigm, challenged their very sense of themselves as professionals and challenged the meaning of their familiar world. After all, if you question such things seriously and openly, you can expect people to feel and express some hostility, because you are in effect denying their identity. It seemed to make more and more sense to assume that the people who reacted so intolerantly to McLuhan's work, called him names and so forth, were using what I will call a linear paradigm, and that McLuhan's nonlinear paradigm struck them as at best confusion, at worst a put on.

By this time I had also discovered the related work of McLuhan's friend and one-time colleague, Walter J. Ong, S.J. Ong's wonderfully articulate studies of the cultural images of sight and sound clarified many general problems to which McLuhan only alluded. I particularly wish to mention *The Presence of the Word,* which helped me in many ways; and Father Ong himself shared his time and wisdom with me on several occasions, as well as in numerous letters.

The organization of this book expresses my tendency to think in analogies. I need to relate one thing—country, art form, or discipline—to another before I can acquire a sense of what it means. Just as I was unable to understand Russian culture without relating it to Southern culture and vice versa, I have found myself unable to understand history without relating it to theoretical assumptions and unable to understand theoretical assumptions without relating them to history. To me, theory grows out of history, and it can then interpret history. In the twentieth century, for instance, the implications of Einsteinian physics have begun to affect all aspects of thought and life, just as the implications of Newtonian physics did in the eighteenth century. As Newtonian physics no longer holds true universally, its implications for philosophy, art, and criticism no longer hold universally.

Since I assume that a nonlinear hypothesis has been gaining in validity in the twentieth century and that this nonlinear paradigm has attained a certain maturity in *Understanding Media,* I employ a two-fold hypothesis in the four parts of this book. I explicate the first aspect of my hypothesis in the first two parts, and the second aspect in the last two parts of the book. Part I, "Paradigms: Linear and Nonlinear," defines the nature of paradigms in detail and states the characteristics of linear and nonlinear paradigms. Part II, "The Growth of the Nonlinear Paradigm," deals with the seminal concepts of art, cognition, and technology that inform *Understanding Media.* As this part shows, McLuhan uses very few completely "original ideas" in his book, for the first half of the twentieth century created an implicit consensus, if only among a small group of people, about these matters. Part III, *"Understanding Media,"* analyzes McLuhan's extraordinary ability to take isolated concepts about which some consensus exists, synthesize them, and apply them to many different kinds of problems. Finally, in Part IV, "The Power of the Paradigm: Some Harmonics of the Implosion Chorus," I assume the validity of my hypothesis, and begin applying analogical reasoning to some problems of twentieth-century culture that have long concerned me.

In addition to the personal, cultural, and intellectual acknowledgments that I have made already, it remains my pleasant duty to acknowledge as well the generous assistance of two institutions that have made this book possible. The American Council of Learned Societies awarded me a fellowship that allowed me to do the time-consuming reading a book like this one requires and to write most of the original longer version of it.[4] Second, the Research Council of the University of Missouri–Columbia awarded me no less than three grants—two of them covered typing costs, and the third paid the necessary permissions fees. I feel great personal gratitude to Dr. X. J. Musacchia, who arranged for these grants.

4. One chapter from the original version appeared in print as "Marshall McLuhan and French Structuralism," *Boundary 2* 1:1 (Fall 1972): 134–46

Contents

Part I.

Paradigms: Linear and Nonlinear

Chapter 1

On the Nature of Paradigms

For the first half of this book, I will be using an adaptation of the term *paradigm* that Thomas B. Kuhn introduced in his *The Structure of Scientific Revolutions* (1962), a work that has attracted a good deal of attention. As the term appears here, it has a more general meaning than it does in Kuhn, because I relate it to its original meaning in linguistics. *Paradigm* thus has something of the function of the term as Berger and Luckmann use it in their *The Social Construction of Reality;* speaking of the social order, they say, "In the establishment of this order language *realizes* a word, in the double sense of apprehending and producing it."[1] However, this chapter will simply explicate Kuhn's use of *paradigm;* the next two chapters will make structural distinctions between the linear and nonlinear paradigms.

Rejecting Bacon's distinction between deduction and induction, Kuhn theorizes that no one can actually use pure deduction and that all perception involves induction of one sort or another. One perceives, so goes his argument, by relating new phenomena to old ones, for past experience leads one to expect their reappearance. It is the system, or structure, of these expectations that Kuhn calls a paradigm.

The significance of expectations becomes strikingly apparent when they fail, as they did when Roentgen discovered X-rays:

> X-rays . . . were greeted not only with surprise but with shock. Lord Kelvin at first pronounced them an elaborate hoax. Others, though they could not doubt the evidence, were clearly staggered by it. Though X-rays were not prohibited by established theory, they violated deeply entrenched expectations. (p.59)[2]

1. Peter L. Berger and Thomas Luckmann, *The Social Construction of Reality,* p. 153.
2. Page numbers after quotations from Kuhn refer to : Thomas B. Kuhn, *The Structure of Scientific Revolutions,* 2d ed., enlarged.

Because expectations play such an important role in perception, as well as in scientific inquiry, psychologists have designed experiments to elicit implicit expectations. Kuhn emphasizes an intriguing experiment that J. S. Bruner and Leo Postman conducted.

> Bruner and Postman asked experimental subjects to identify on short and controlled exposure a series of playing cards. Many of the cards were normal, but some were made anomalous, e.g., a red six of spades and a black four of hearts. Each experimental run was constituted by the display of a single card to a single subject in a series of gradually increased exposures. . . . The anomalous cards were almost always identified, without apparent hesitation or puzzlement, as normal. . . . Without any awareness of trouble, it was immediately fitted to one of the conceptual categories prepared by prior experience. One would not even like to say that the subjects had seen something different from what they identified. (pp. 62–63)

After discussing the experiment, Kuhn concludes:

> Either as a metaphor or because it reflects the nature of the mind, that psychological experiment provides a wonderfully simple and cogent scheme for the process of scientific discovery. In science, as in the playing card experiment, novelty emerges only with difficulty manifested by resistance, against a background provided by expectation. Initially, only the anticipated and usual are experienced even under circumstances where anomaly is later to be observed. Further acquaintance, however, does result in awareness of something wrong or does relate the effect to something that has gone wrong before. That awareness of anomaly opens a period in which conceptual categories are adjusted until the initially anomalous has become the anticipated. (p. 64)

There seems to be little doubt, then, that expectations give a key to the nature of paradigms, and thus to perception; keeping this essential fact in mind, let us consider some specific issues in the argument that Kuhn develops.

Kuhn begins Chapter 3, "The Nature of Normal Science," ("Normal science" is the practice of a scientific community which shares a paradigm), with his most explicit definition of a paradigm.

> In its established usage, a paradigm is an accepted model or pattern, and that aspect of its meaning has enabled me, lacking

a better word, to appropriate 'paradigm' here. But it will shortly be clear that the sense of 'model' and 'pattern' that permits that appropriation is not quite the usual one in defining 'paradigm'. In grammar, for example, *'amo, amas, amat'* is a paradigm because it displays the pattern to be used in conjugating a large number of other Latin verbs, e.g. in producing *'laudo, laudas, laudat.'* In this standard application, the paradigm functions by permitting the replication of examples any one of which could in principle serve to replace it. In a science, on the other hand, a paradigm is rarely an object for replication. Instead, like an accepted judicial decision in common law, it is an object for further articulation and specification under new or more stringent conditions. (p. 23)

Kuhn notes that in science, as in language, one need not have the capacity to articulate a paradigm in order to use it.

Scientists work from models acquired through education and through subsequent exposure to the literature often without quite knowing or needing to know what characteristics have given these models the status of community paradigms. (p. 136)

But Kuhn wants to discuss not so much the success of a paradigm as its failure; this failure, in extreme form, precipitates the kind of scientific revolutions that we associate with the names of Newton and Einstein.

To understand what happens during such a revolution, one should note Kuhn's observation that no paradigm solves, or ever can solve, *all* the problems that it poses; an area of what Kuhn calls "creative tension" exists. When this creative tension becomes excessive, it means that the paradigm has failed, and those within the community begin to examine it, for they sense that the distinctions between interpretation and description retain little of their meaning. Kuhn analyzes those distinctions in the following way:

Rather than being elementary logical or methodological distinctions, which would thus be prior to the analysis of scientific knowledge, they [distinctions between interpretation and description] now seem integral parts of a traditional set of substantive answers to the very questions upon which they have been deployed. That circularity does not at all invalidate them. But it does make them parts of a theory and, in doing so, subjects them to the same scrutiny regularly applied to theories in other fields. (p. 9)

This circularity causes the extreme tension that occurs when paradigms conflict; the adherents of each paradigm find justification on their own terms.

> To the extent, as significant as it is incomplete, that two scientific schools disagree about what is a problem and what a solution, they will inevitably talk through each other when debating the relative merits of their respective paradigms. (p. 109)

Because of this lack of communication between paradigms, "The transfer of allegiance [from one paradigm to another] is a conversion experience that cannot be forced" (p. 151).

Because this conversion experience changes the scientist's perception, Kuhn believes that the history of science is not cumulative (as people usually think of it), but discontinuous, for no connection joins the old and the new paradigm.

> Led by a new paradigm, scientists adopt new instruments and look in new places. Even more important, during revolutions scientists see new and different things when looking with familiar instruments in places they have looked before. (p. 111)

> . . . Though the world does not change with a change of paradigm, the scientist afterward works in a different world . . . I am convinced that we must learn to make sense of statements that at least resemble these. What occurs during a scientific revolution is not fully reducible to a reinterpretation of individual and stable data. (p. 121)

Kuhn himself is aware of the problems and deficiencies in his presentation, which is at least equally important for what it does not say as for what it does say. Nevertheless, I have let him speak for himself. But I wish to distinguish my own use of the concept of a paradigm from his seminal discussion. Generally speaking, I believe that Kuhn has applied to scientific inquiry a general fact of human perception to which he has given too little theoretical attention.

Discussions of *The Structure of Scientific Revolutions* with acquaintances familiar with the book suggest that they usually understand the concept of a paradigm as a reference to one of several methodologies which one can choose and discard at will. Whatever the merits of this interpretation, I will not use it here, nor does Kuhn himself use it. No one can casually choose or reject a paradigm, because "Something like a paradigm is prerequisite to perception itself" (p. 113). No one ever discusses the paradigm itself, under conditions of "normal science," because it is the paradigm that makes discussion possible at all. To avoid confusion about this point, let us turn to a familiar situation that starkly illustrates the nature of a paradigm: a football game.

Sports provide exceptionally useful illustrations, because their paradigms are explicitly and more or less permanently codified in easily accessible rule books. For example, the regulation football field is one hundred yards long. Without a field of this length, no official game can take place. Yet if we examine the offense in football, we find that coaches at various times have used very different styles and formations. The single wing, the *T*-formation, the split *T*-formation, the *I*-formation, and numerous variations of these would appear on any list. These offenses express different philosophies of football and use different plays; a good defense will respond to each offensive formation with a different formation of its own, and so forth. Yet *all* these formations, both offensive and defensive, presume the presence of the hundred-yard field. The coaches never mention this fact during their pep talks at half-time, nor do the announcers at games broadcast on radio and television mention it; they rightly assume that everybody knows that the field is one hundred yards long. That which "everybody knows," and *which therefore makes the game possible,* is what constitutes a paradigm.

Football also illustrates the capacity of a paradigm to combine arbitrariness and meaningfulness. There is no inherent reason that a football field *must* be one hundred years long (in Canada, it is ten yards longer); yet this arbitrarily defined area provides the setting for the intense emotion that thousands of people experience on weekends during the fall.

Although it does not normally occur to a football fan to mention the length of the field, he does have a conscious knowledge of this and the other rules of the game, and this matter of conscious knowledge shows the limitations of the analogy between paradigms and rules for sports. Except under very unusual conditions, those who use the paradigms of science which interest Kuhn and those who use the more general paradigms which interest me cannot articulate them. Usually the very fact that an individual can make certain statements excludes those statements from paradigmatic status, because he or she has to use the paradigm to make them.

Thus, conflicts among paradigms can become personal crises. To become a creative scholar, or—more generally—to exist in a society one must internalize its most pervasive paradigm, and make it part of one's inmost being. When a scientific or cultural revolution replaces one paradigm with another, and creates a new world, those who have completely internalized the old paradigm may find it emotionally impossible to change their thought patterns, and thus have deeply personal reasons for opposing the new theory. Rudolf Carnap, in his *Philosophical Foundations of Physics,* recounts a poignant anecdote of a man caught precisely in this situation.

> I remember an occasion, about 1930, when I discussed relativity with a German physicist in Prague. He was extremely depressed. "This is terrible," he said. "Look what Einstein has done to our wonderful physics."
>
> "Terrible?" I replied. I was enthusiastic about the new physics. With only a few general principles describing a certain types of invariance and the exciting adoption of non-Euclidean geometry so much could be explained that had been unintelligible before! But this physicist had so strong an emotional resistance to theories difficult to visualize that he had almost lost his enthusiasm for physics because of Einstein's revolutionary changes. The only thing that sustained him was the hope that some day—and he hoped it would be during his lifetime—a counterrevolutionary leader would come to restore the old classical order, in which he could breathe more comfortably and feel at home again.[3]

Carnap's German physicist, whose counterparts are legion in the twentieth century, experienced intense anxiety, for he had lost an essential aspect of his belief in himself. The anxiety is all the more excruciating, because mere reasoning cannot bring about a change from a linear to a nonlinear paradigm. To cite Kuhn on this point:

> Paradigms are not corrigible by normal science at all. Instead, as we have already seen, normal science ultimately leads only to the recognition of anomalies and crises. And these are terminated, not by deliberation and interpretation, but by a

3. Rudolph Carnap, *Philosophical Foundations of Physics,* Martin Gardner, ed., pp. 173–74.

relatively sudden and unstructured event like the gestalt switch. Scientists then often speak of the "scales falling from the eyes" or of the "lightning flash" that "inundates" a previously obscure puzzle, enabling its components to be seen in a new way that for the first time permits its solution. (p. 122)

But those who undergo what Kuhn calls the "gestalt switch" also experience great tension, for they must find someone to whom they can communicate what they perceive.

If a paradigm is ever to triumph it must gain some first supporters, men who will develop it to the point where hardheaded arguments can be produced and multiplied. . . . Something must make at least a few scientists feel that the new proposal is on the right track, and sometimes it is only personal and inarticulate aesthetic considerations that can do that. Men have been converted by them at times when most of the articulable technical arguments pointed the other way. When first introduced, neither Copernicus' astronomical theory nor De Broglie's theory of matter had many other significant grounds of appeal. Even today Einstein's general theory attracts men principally on aesthetic grounds, an appeal that few people outside of mathematics have been able to feel. (p. 158)

I belong among those to whom the nonlinear paradigm of *Understanding Media* appeals primarily because of "aesthetic considerations," but I propose to develop "hardheaded arguments" to validate it. In dealing with society, however, it is notoriously more difficult to articulate one's principles than in science. The difficulties in communication that occur between paradigms make it imperative to attempt to do so in unemotional terms. Thus in developing the arguments of the next two chapters, I will be using *paradigm* in a manner that draws on a principle that the American logician Willard Quine states in his essay "Ontological Relativity."

Quine assumes that all discourse depends on what he calls a "background language," which functions in the following way:

It is meaningless to ask whether, in general, our terms "rabbit," "rabbit part," "number," etc., really refer respectively to rabbits, rabbit parts, number, etc., rather than to some ingeniously permuted denotations. It is meaningless to ask this absolutely; we can meaningfully ask it only relative to some background language. When we ask, "Does 'rabbit' really refer to rabbits?" someone can counter with the question: "Refer to rabbits in what sense of 'rabbits'?" thus launching a regress; and we need the background language to regress into. The background language gives the query sense, if only relative sense; sense relative in turn to it, this background language.[4]

Likewise, I will be using the term *paradigm* relative to a background language. In the next two chapters I will use as background languages for the linear and nonlinear paradigms the physics of Newton and Einstein respectively (as Milič Čapek describes them in *The Philosophical Impact of Contemporary Physics*[5]). (The phrase "the linear paradigm" will refer to the set of all possible linear paradigms and the phrase "the nonlinear paradigm" will refer to the set of all possible nonlinear paradigms; "a linear paradigm" or "a nonlinear paradigm" will refer to an individual member of the set.) In keeping with Kuhn's usage, I assume that each set of paradigms creates its own problems and its own means of solving them; moreover, each set employs its own images. The matter of images in expository prose (and in everyday speech, for that matter) will concern us greatly, for I wish to paraphrase Sartre's "A technique always implies a metaphysics" as "An image always implies a physics." One particular image recurs in the use of each paradigm—the line in the linear paradigm, and the circle in the nonlinear paradigm. Their appearance thus has epistemological import.

4. Willard Van Orman Quine, "Ontological Relativity," in *Ontological Relativity and Other Essays,* pp. 48–49.
5. Milič Čapek, *The Philosophical Impact of Contemporary Physics.*

Chapter 2

The Linear Paradigm

The passages in Čapek's discussion of Newtonian, or "classical," physics that have immediate relevance for the nature of the linear paradigm involve concepts of space, time, and matter. Let us begin with space.

> In classical science space was regarded as a homogeneous medium existing objectively and independently of its physical content, whose rigid and timeless structure has been described by the axioms and theorems of Euclidean geometry. This self-sufficiency of space and its independence of the matter which it contains was clearly formulated by Newton in his *Principia:* "Absolute space, in its own nature, without regard to anything external, remains always similar and immovable."[1]

Classical physics integrates its concept of space with that of time in the following manner.

> Time is the second fundamental concept of classical physics. While space was defined as the three-dimensional manifold of coexisting homogeneous terms, time was regarded as the one-dimensional manifold of successive terms. The basic relation in space is juxtaposition; the basic relation in time is *succession.* The points of space are *beside* one another; the instants of time *follow* one another. While we keep this fundamental difference in mind, we can apply a large part of what has just been said about space to time as well. Both space and time were regarded as species of manifold, and both were believed to share the property of being homogeneous. As in the case of space, the basic attributes of time followed from its homogeneity: its independence of its physical content, its infinity, continuity, and uniformity. The uniformity of time was a

1. Milič Čapek, *The Philosophical Impact of Contemporary Physics,* p. 7.

counterpart of the immutability of space; it might be more expressively designated *uniform fluidity.* [2]

These concepts of space and time have various epistemological implications. For example, the very word *objectivity* implies its opposite, subjectivity; these two concepts form a dichotomy, in which one term excludes the other. No single trait more distinctly characterizes the linear paradigm than its tendency to set up such dichotomies. Additional examples, such as rationality–irrationality, and good–evil will readily occur to the reader. As these three sets of examples suggest, linear paradigms place an implicit value judgment on one term of the dichotomy.

The existence of objective time and space implies the existence of objective truth. In an extreme form, the linear paradigm construes truth as admitting no gradations or ambiguities; like being, Truth is what it is, and nothing else. This concept of truth has the same nature as the concept of matter in classical physics:

> The third basic entity of the world of classical physics was *matter.* This concept has hardly changed from the times of Leucippus to the beginning of the twentieth century: an impenetrable *something* which fills completely certain regions of space and which persists through time even when it changes its location. . . .
> . . . The empirical fact of motion led the early atomists to admit the existence of *empty space* or *void.* . . . This conclusion was adopted not only by all later atomists but also, . . . by all classical scientists, who clearly realized that the denial of empty space and the reality of motion can be only verbally reconciled. . . . If matter is full space, then its constitutive elements must be by their own nature impenetrable, indivisible, indestructible, rigid, and homogeneous. [3]

Since the linear paradigm construes the universe as having everywhere and always the arrangement of a piece of graph paper (with the

2. Ibid., p. 35. Čapek's emphasis, here and elsewhere. Cf. the following etymological analysis by the Swiss scholar Jean Gebser, which substantiates what Čapek says here: "All the words of our language which mean 'time—German 'Zeit,' English 'time,' Latin 'tempus,' as well as French 'temps,' and so on—go back to the Indo-Germanic root 'do.' This root, in Ionian, the original language of Greek philosophy, means 'to separate, to divide, to split up, to tear apart, to mangle.'" Jean Gebser, *Ursprung und Gegenwart,* 1:276.

3. Ibid., pp. 54–55.

difference that the universe has three dimensions, not two), those who use a linear paradigm speak of events that occur "in" objective, neutral space and time. Since a universe composed of objective space and time has an objective existence, as does the rigid matter "in" it, one finds truth by examining that which the universe contains—content. One who assumes, consciously or unconsciously, that the universe everywhere and always retains its rigidity and homogeneity has little need to concern himself with form, for he can assume it as invariant. In the linear paradigm, the truth that one finds by examining content partakes of the objective nature of matter. Hence the phrase "to discover truth," a phrase that compares truth to an island that exists independently of the discoverer.

"To discover" means "to dis-cover": to remove the cover of something and thus make it visible. In general, the linear paradigm employs spatialized, visual imagery; the terms make a single reference, since one sees that which is fixed in homogeneous Newtonian space. Thus, Čapek refers to:

> The precept which John Tyndal recommended in his Liverpool
> address to the physicists of the Victorian era as a reliable
> criterion of satisfactory scientific theories: "Ask your imagination
> if it will accept it," i.e., ask yourself if you are able to draw a
> mental picture of the phenomenon in question; reject it if no
> visual diagram, no mechanical model can be constructed. This
> demand hardly varied from the seventeenth to the nineteenth
> century; Tyndal's recommendation is basically the same as that
> of Descartes and Huygens. . . . From the epistemological point
> of view this is probably the most significant and revealing trait
> of the classical theories.[4]

Walter Ong's explication of the term *world view* shows that visual imagery appears not only in science but in philosophy as well.

> However we break it down or specify it, the term "world view"
> suggests some sort of major unifying perception, and it presents
> the unification as taking place in a visual field. "View" implies
> sight, directly and analogously. The concept is of a piece with
> many other spatially grounded metaphors we commonly avail
> ourselves of in treating perception and understanding: "Areas"
> of study; "fields" of investigation, "levels" of abstraction,

4. Ibid., p. 4.

"fronts" of knowledge, "waves" of interest, "movements" of
ideas and so on indefinitely.[5]

The vocabulary of the literary critic presents a large number of visual,
spatialized metaphors. In order to "fill a gap" in our knowledge by
"arriving at" an "objective view," the critic may choose a new "approach" by subjecting the author's character "portrayals" to "scrutiny," or by "focusing" on them. He may read the work of the author's
contemporaries so as to "place" him in historical "perspective." If he
considers himself innovative, he may "move in a new direction" and
"explore" new "areas"; if historically inclined, he speaks of "land-
marks," "milestones," and "turning points." Indeed, our society as a
whole assumes that visual images create effective explanations. We
read in newspapers that governments adopt diplomatic "postures,"
that hopes for peace "rise" and "fall," that charities urge us to "stamp
out" cancer; and disc jockeys tell us that they will bring us the news
"at the top of the hour." (These examples should of course make it
clear that the term *visual image* corresponds roughly to what Marx
called a "reification.")

I have stressed the visual images of the linear paradigm because
for most people images play the role that a model plays in scientific
inquiry. They mediate between the unconsciously assumed paradigm
and the immediate situation. Or, as John Graves puts it, "It [the model]
points to analogies or isomorphisms between the known and the
unknown (or imperfectly known)."[6] The visual images of the linear
paradigm express its propensity to use sight as the dominant and
sufficient mode of perception, and thus to perceive phenomena as
isolates. An inadequate awareness of the implications of imagery
weakens arguments, for imagery can create a structure that does not
correspond to the one the author intends.

Kuhn himself provides an example when he writes, "To make the
transition to Einstein's universe, the whole conceptual web whose
strands are space, time, matter, force, and so on, has to be shifted and
laid down again on nature whole" (p. 149). Not only are the strands
of a web discrete; unlike the concepts of "space, time, matter, force,
and so on," they do not have, in scientific practice, any distinction

5. Walter J. Ong, S. J., "World as View and World as Event," *American
Anthropologist* 71:4 (August, 1969), p. 635.

6. John Graves, *The Conceptual Foundations of Contemporary Relativity Theory*, p. 48.

from "nature." While Kuhn wants most of all to demonstrate the *inseparability* of scientific concepts from nature, his imagery denies it. As Graves would put it, he fails to create an isomorphism between known and unknown. The point is not a minor one, for most of the problems that critics have noted in Kuhn's presentation, such as a lack of clarity in using the term *paradigm,* actually derive from his attempt to present a nonvisual theory by means of visual images.

To return to Newton, objective space has still other implications in the linear paradigm. Čapek says of Newtonian space that it "has been described by the axioms and theorems of Euclidean geometry." This statement draws our attention to the axiomatic method of reasoning, which Euclid used.

> The axiomatic method consists in accepting *without* proof certain propositions as axioms of postulates (e.g., the axiom that through two points just one straight line can be drawn), and then deriving from the axioms all other propositions as theorems. The axioms constitute the "foundations" of the systems; the theorems are the "superstructure," and are obtained from the axioms with the exclusive help of logic.[7]

The linear paradigm has transferred the axiomatic method—a conceptual equivalent of objective space—from Euclidean geometry and Newtonian physics, to its reasoning about other matters; here again, imagery provides important evidence. Anyone who "bases," "grounds," or "founds" a theory, an argument, or whatever, is using the axiomatic method; the very idea of a base implies the static quality of the Newtonian universe and the separation of theory and practice, or facts and interpretation.

Among the theorems of Euclidean geometry is one that states that a line is continuous and one that states that a line consists of an infinite number of points. It is possible to characterize the opposition of these two theorems as a dichotomy, and to define that dichotomy as essential in the linear paradigm, according to which the set of all linear paradigms divides into two subsets, which we may call the continuous and the noncontinuous subsets.

Those who use the continuous subset of linear paradigms emphasize that in Čapek's terms, in the Newtonian universe the basic relation in time is succession, and thus the mathematical continuity of time follows with logical force from its homogeneity. They conclude that

7. Ernest Nagel and James R. Newman, *Gödel's Proof,* p. 5.

any phenomenon, work, or individual derives meaning from its position on a line. The idea that a concept, a theme in literature, or a political trend has a continuous history (and thus exists in objective space) appears very clearly in the interest in tracing—another unconscious visual image that implies a line—its evolution. (Obviously, much of nineteenth-century thought uses the continuous subset of the linear paradigm.) Thus, any large library has a number of books whose titles begin with phrases such as "The Origins of . . . ," "The Rise of . . . ," and "The Sources of. . . ."

The continuous subset also attributes considerable importance to "tracing" influences. An inherently geometrical idea that two phenomena constitute discrete lines in objective space, and that influence occurs at the point of intersection, makes possible the study of influence. For people who reason in this way, an artist may derive his distinction not so much from his work in itself as from the influence which he exerts. When Igor Stravinsky died, news reports identified him as "the most influential composer of the twentieth century." That is to say, Stravinsky's work constitutes a line that intersects with more lines than any other composer's.

In the continuous subset of the linear paradigm, space may so predominate that the situation that Čapek calls "The Implicit Elimination of Time in Classical Physics" results. Čapek's argument goes as follows:

> Any instantaneous configuration of an isolated system logically implies all future configurations of the system. Its future history is thus virtually contained in its present state, which, in its turn is logically contained in its past states. What is true of any isolated system must be true of the whole universe, provided that the universe itself possesses the character of an isolated system. The last supposition was more or less tacitly accepted in the classical science.[8]

Thus, all forms of determinism imply a linear paradigm, because they all involve the belief that a process occurs along a predetermined, predictable line. In making time everything, determinism in fact makes it irrelevant.

Lest confusion arise about the linear quality of determinism, I wish to add that free will is an equally linear concept. It simply belongs to the other subset of the linear paradigm, the noncontinuous subset.

8. Čapek, *Philosophical Impact of Contemporary Physics,* p. 122.

state that physical reality changes with time."[5]

If "only the event itself" has reality, reality is not static, and one cannot easily visualize it. Therefore, as a heuristic device in this book, I propose to create a coherence between theory and imagery by heeding Čapek's assertion that: "A radical abandonment of visual and imaginative models in modern physics is absolutely imperative if the meaning of the present crisis in physics is not to escape us entirely."[6] Although the practice may prove too programmatic to use continually, I propose to use aural images for the nonlinear paradigm, and visual images for the linear paradigm. Čapek's argument for the use of musical imagery in a paradigm that emphasizes intrinsic historicity strikes me as most compelling:

> The musical phrase is a *successive differentiated whole* which remains a whole in spite of its successive character and which remains differentiated in spite of its dynamic wholeness. . . . Every musical structure is by its own nature unfolding and incomplete; so is cosmic becoming, the time-space of modern physics. The musical structures, in virtue of their essentially temporal nature, cannot be subdivided *ad infinitum* without being destroyed; they are, as Ehrenfels pointed out long ago, *zeitliche Gestalten* [temporal structures] whose duration is their existential minimum, which cannot be shortened without being destroyed.[7]

Only in the discussion of media in the Part III of this book will it become possible to make explicit the full meaning of this relationship between sound and the nonlinear paradigm.

If "only the event" has reality, of what do events consist? The famous equation $E = mc^2$ gives a helpful answer, since it states that mass has no inherent permanence and that energy constitutes the essential element of the universe. Since matter can undergo transformations into energy and a different kind of matter, processes consist of energy transformations, and a rich nonlinear paradigm will define itself in terms of such transformations. Rather like a physicist analyzing tracks in a bubble chamber, those who use a nonlinear paradigm in

5. André Mercier, "Knowledge and Physical Reality," *Physics, Logic, and History,* Wolfgang Yourgrau and Allen D. Breck, eds., p. 49.
6. Čapek, *The Philosophical Impact of Contemporary Physics,* p. 235.
7. Ibid., pp. 371–73.

investigating society will treat cultural artifacts as manifestations of energy transformations.

The energy in the atom is electricity, of course, and in his thoughtful, perceptive book, *Doubt and Certainty in Science,* the British biologist J. Z. Young remarks, "Electricity is the condition we observe when there are certain spatial relations between things—when a wire is moved near a magnet or when chemicals are properly arranged in a battery."[8] Electrical energy occurs when there are "certain spatial relationships between things," most simply between positive and negative poles. This relationship creates a decisive, recurrent concept in the nonlinear paradigm: binarism.

The nonlinear paradigm resolves the dichotomies of the linear paradigm into binary pairs, which interact and each term of which is equally necessary. Thus the value judgments inherent in using dichotomies have little significance in a nonlinear paradigm. Unlike the linear paradigm's treatment of, say, good and evil as opposites placed at the extremes of a line, the nonlinear paradigm considers that only good and evil together can form a whole. One recognizes the nature of each member of the pair through the contrast which its opposite creates.

It seems important to distinguish the irrelevance of value judgments in the nonlinear paradigm from the linear concept of "value-free" social science, which purports to flatten its material into a static, homogeneous field. Not only does the difference between the linear and the nonlinear paradigms amount to a difference between stasis and dynamism, but also the dynamism of the nonlinear paradigm derives from the way a function mediates between the members of the pair. I cannot develop this abstruse point here, but I mention it in order to clarify the nature of binarism.

One should probably consider binarism the most important, pervasive, and fruitful, concept of the twentieth century.[9] I should therefore like to discuss here three essential binary pairs in the nonlinear paradigm, which I propose to develop: structure–discontinuity, fruitfulness–barrenness, and causality–arbitrariness.

One may relate the idea of structure to electricity, which pro-

8. J. Z. Young, *Doubt and Certainty in Science,* p. 109.
9. For an informative but schematic presentation of many of the uses of binarism in twentieth-century theory, see Walter Bloch, *Polarität.* In a different vein, there is a suspense thriller which incorporates binarism into the plot: John Lange, *Binary.*

duces a field in which force, magnitude, and so on, will depend solely on the local situation. Hence, the nonlinear paradigm will concern itself with fields, which form structured totalities, or wholes. Yet holistic methodologies often encounter the objection that if one proposes to work with wholes, one must work with the universe, or nothing. Since one manifestly cannot deal with the universe, the argument continues, one cannot deal with anything at all. However, this argument (readily recognizable now as a dichotomy) presupposes a continuous homogeneous universe that contains the possibility of infinite regression, and it ceases to have any force once we understand that in a binary system structure implies discontinuity. Čapek makes the point very well:

> It is true that during the process of absorption of radiation an electron (still speaking in terms of Bohr's model) "jumps" from an orbit of smaller radius to one of a larger radius, whereas during the process of emission it "jumps" in an opposite direction; but it soon became evident that a continuous spatio-temporal description of such "jumps" is impossible; there was no experimental way to determine the hypothetical positions of a jumping electron in the interval separating two orbits.[10]

Electrons move either in one orbit or another; one cannot speak of the transition from one orbit to another precisely because of the discontinuity of space. Discontinuity also appears in the energy levels of the excited states of atoms when one bombards them with electrons in an atomic accelerator; these levels do not increase gradually and continuously, but exhibit distinct, discontinuous states that give measurements in simple fractions.

For work with sociocultural problems, the opposition of structure and discontinuity has important procedural implications. As a practical matter, structure can exist as part of a larger whole yet also be discontinuous or autonomous with respect to it. While this principle may seem an ad hoc formulation, the work of ecologists has given cogent justification for it.

> No level [of organization] in an ecological community is any more or less important, or any more or less deserving of scientific study than any other level. . . . *When we consider the unique characteristics which develop at each level,* there is no

10. Čapek, *The Philosophical Impact of Contemporary Physics,* p. 235.

reason to suppose that any level is any more difficult or any easier to study quantitatively. . . . Furthermore, the findings at any one level *aid in the study of another level, but never completely explain the phenomena at that level.*[11]

When applied to society, these remarks suggest that large systems consist of multiplicities of smaller systems, any of which may be validly investigated independently of all others.

In a way, the binary pair barrenness–fruitfulness merely gives a specific instance of the pair discontinuity–structure. A nonlinear paradigm that has an elegant structure can, and will, prove fruitful in dealing with many kinds of problems—but not with all. *No paradigm can solve all problems,* and this situation depends neither on its state of development nor on the skill of the user. Thus, to pose a problem that the proponent of a particular paradigm cannot solve does not necessarily prove the paradigm invalid. Incidentally, although Kuhn does not use the term *binarism,* he implies the barrenness–fruitfulness pair when he speaks of the "area of creative tension" in all paradigms. (Note here again Kuhn's use of a spatialized metaphor.)

This reference to Kuhn makes it convenient to use a typical reaction to *The Structure of Scientific Revolutions* as a way of introducing the pair causality–arbitrariness. In a volume devoted to Kuhn's work, the British scientist J. W. N. Watkins referred to "Kuhn's view of scientific normalcy as a closed society of closed minds."[12] Presumably, Watkins is thinking here of one of Kuhn's statements, such as: "An apparently arbitrary element, compounded of personal and historical accident, is always a formative ingredient of the beliefs espoused by a given scientific community at a given time" (p. 4). Watkins's objection obviously uses a linear paradigm, which excludes the possibility of binarism, because—in a manner typical of people who think in dichotomies—he takes Kuhn's emphasis on the arbitrary quality of binarism as its *only* quality. He takes Kuhn to be saying that arbitrariness totally and exhaustively defines science, and anyone who

11. Eugene P. Odum, with Howard T. Odum, *Fundamentals of Ecology,* p. 7. Odum's emphasis.

12. J. W. N. Watkins, "Against 'Normal Science,' " in *Criticism and the Growth of Knowledge,* eds. Imre Lakatos and Alan Musgrave. Imre Lakatos feels so threatened by Kuhn's nonlinear paradigm that in an article with such a formal title as "Falsification and the Methodology of Scientific Research Programmes" he can deliver himself of the following remark: "Kuhn's position would vindicate, no doubt, the basic political *credo* of contemporary religious maniacs ('student revolutionaries')." Ibid., p. 93.

believes this must believe that science has no meaning.

In fact, of course, Kuhn is merely emphasizing the arbitrary quality of cognition, in order to counterbalance those who use a linear paradigm and believe only in its determined quality (i.e., that it describes something "out there"). Had Kuhn had a binary view of the nature of perception, he could more readily have explained why scientists live in a "different world" after a "Gestalt switch." They live in a different world (as do individuals after intense religious experiences, which partake of the same nature as Kuhn's "Gestalt switch") because the interaction of the causal and arbitrary components of perception has undergone a restructuring.

I believe that this discussion of the epistemological implications of binarism may create the possibility of beginning a resolution of a group of the most baffling problems in twentieth-century intellectual history. These problems occur in metalogic (talk about the nature of logic). Three mathematicians have particular importance for metalogic —Kurt Gödel, Thoral Skolem, and Alonzo Church. Although those of us who have not done advanced work in mathematical logic will never manage even to state their theorems rigorously, we can use these paraphrases that Howard Delong has supplied:

1. *Gödel's first incompleteness theorem* (generalized version): There exists a predicate such that there is no correct and complete formal system for it.

2. *Church's theorem* (generalized version): There exists a predicate such that there is no correct formal system which contains a decision procedure for both the predicate and its negation.

3. *Skolem's theorem* (generalized version): There is no consistent, categorical formal system having the natural numbers as its intended interpretation.[13]

13. Howard Delong, *A Profile of Mathematical Logic,* p. 195. Perhaps the discipline necessary for working in advanced logic precludes an awareness of the role of science and mathematics as epistemological disciplines; whether for this reason or some other, the titles of the principal articles on metalogic promise more than their texts deliver. Stephen Korner's article "On the Relevance of Post-Godelian Mathematics to Philosophy" (in *Problems in the Philosophy of Mathematics,* Imre Lakatos, ed., pp. 118–32) turns out to be too bland and general to stimulate further work. J. R. Lucas has written "Minds, Machines, and Gödel," probably the best-known article on the problem *(Philosophy);* Lucas proposes to refute mechanism, i.e., the linear paradigm, with Gödel's Proof, but he lacks the necessary theoretical terminology, and his

If we set aside the details (as laymen must do in any case) and begin with a general description, Gödel's Theorem (and by implication, the other two as well) will become comprehensible and meaningful, if not utilizable in a technical sense. One can say that, essentially, Gödel proved invalid the axiomatic method that Euclid and Newton used.

> [Gödel] presented mathematicians with the astounding and melancholy conclusion that the axiomatic method has certain inherent limitations, which rule out the possibility that even the ordinary arithmetic of the integers can ever be fully axiomatized. What is more, he proved that it is impossible to establish the internal logical consistency of a very large class of deductive systems—elementary arithmetic, for example—unless one adopts principles of reasoning so complex that their internal consistency is as open to doubt as that of the systems themselves. In light of these conclusions, no final systematization of many important areas of mathematics is attainable, and no absolutely impeccable guarantee can be given that many significant branches of mathematical thought are entirely free from internal contradiction.[14]

Just as Einstein resolved homogeneous space and time into process, so Gödel resolved Euclid's axioms into dynamic cognitive structures. One must conclude that consistent systems are not complete, and that complete systems are not consistent. After Gödel's work

> in order to create a theory in the sense of showing its non-contradiction, it no longer sufficed to analyze its presuppositions but it becomes necessary to construct the following theory. Previously, one could consider theories as forming a neat pyramid resting on a self-sufficient base, the bottom level being the most solid because it was formed by the simplest means. But if simplicity becomes a sign of weakness

article has understandably evoked a good deal of opposition. Lucas relies on purely verbal arguments to resolve a problem that related both to mathematics and physiology, but since he fails to bring the conceptual rigor of either discipline to his discussion, it leaves the impression of a scholastic treatise that lacks the orienting tradition of the church fathers. Judson Webb's "Metamathematics and the Philosophy of Mind" *(Philosophy of Science)* may represent the opposition to Lucas's article here; Webb seems willfully obscure, and, ultimately flatly denies the possibility of a relationship between mathematics and epistemology.

14. Ernest Nagel and James R. Newman, *Gödel's Proof,* p. 6.

and in order to consolidate a level one must construct the following one, the consistency of the pyramid is in reality suspended from its summit and from a summit which it never reaches and which is constantly rising: the image of the pyramid thus needs to be reversed and, more precisely, replaced by that of a spiral the radius of whose turns grows larger and larger as it rises.[15]

In a nonlinear paradigm that has no visual, spatialized images, one would not "envisage" human knowledge as a building or anything else; and because of the dynamic quality of processes, no one can "found," "base," or "support" them.

Now a spiral both rises and turns upon itself; it thus has a kind of binary quality. Gödel's cognitive spiral therefore can be seen as realizing in its form the binary pair causality–arbitrariness. Since systems can be complete or consistent, but not both, one can choose consistency and consciously accept the resultant incompleteness and arbitrariness as logical and natural.

The principles of the nonlinear paradigm, which have received a deliberately sketchy treatment here, construe the universe as a reflexive process of energy transformation. This process has many autonomous structural levels, and it occurs through the opposition of binary poles. To achieve the necessary degree of abstraction for this statement, I have had to give up much of the necessary historical context. I will remedy this in the next part of the book. However, I can anticipate my arguments by quoting Delong, whose adherence to mathematical rigor compels him to state: "Any fixed comprehensive account of reality which states its own truth-conditions could not possibly be true, but only mythical or fictional. *No non-poetic account of the totality of which we are a part can be adequate.*"[16]

15. Jean Piaget, *Le Structuralisme,* pp. 30–31.
16. Delong, *A Profile of Mathematical Logic,* p. 227. My emphasis.

Part II

The Growth of the Nonlinear Paradigm

Chapter **4**

Unconscious Collaborators

Kuhn says in "Postscript—1969," "If this book were being re-written, it would . . . open with a discussion of the community structure of science" (p. 176). He also introduces a helpful definition, and a suggestion.

> A paradigm governs, in the first instance, not a subject matter but rather a group of practitioners. Any study of paradigm-directed or paradigm-shattering research must begin by locating the responsible group or groups. (p. 180)

In this part of the book, I wish to identify "a group of practitioners," who helped to create or articulate various aspects of the nonlinear paradigm that appears in *Understanding Media*. To some extent, the individuals whom I discuss here have worked in isolation and have arrived at similar attitudes independent of the others' work. (This especially applies to those who have discussed technology.) To validate a conceptual paradigm, which does not lend itself to demonstrations in a laboratory, one needs to demonstrate that shared attitudes do prevail among a group of practitioners. Whether or not the practitioners have an awareness that they share these attitudes matters very little.

The creation of a rich new paradigm probably depends on the previous creation of a number of other innovative paradigms that serve, in one way or another, as components. (The obvious example is the role of non-Euclidean geometry in the development of relativity theory.) An examination of *Understanding Media* in the context of modernist art and theory suggests that it draws on and synthesizes some of the nonlinear paradigms of modernism in various creative ways. Thus, in order to demonstrate the validity of the paradigm of *Understanding Media,* one needs to demonstrate the validity of the relevant nonlinear paradigms.

Western thinkers who have used a nonlinear paradigm have tended to make generally similar assumptions about society, art, phi-

31

losophy, and technology. These assumptions are so stimulating, however, that one can develop them at great length. Nonlinear thought has
found particularly strong expression in Germany, as the following
remarks by H. Stuart Hughes make clear:

> In the dominant Anglo-French tradition, the primacy of sense
> perception [i.e., vision] and the validity of empirical procedures
> were taken for granted as naturally as the supremacy of
> "ideas" was accepted in Germany. And from these
> assumptions there followed certain familiar consequences:
> utilitarianism and positivism, democracy and natural science, in
> Britain and France became logical sets of partners. In Germany
> it was otherwise.[1]

It was especially otherwise in Germany in the first two decades of the
nineteenth century. In German romantic thought we find clear antici-
pations of the nonlinear paradigm of modernism. By noticing a few of
these, and by remembering the differences between what Hughes
calls "the dominant Anglo-French tradition" and that of Germany, we
may acquire a helpful sense of modernism's relation to romanticism.

René Wellek writes, with regard to romanticism:

> We can speak of romantic criticism as the establishment of a
> dialectical and symbolistic view of poetry. It grows out of the
> organic analogy, developed by Herder and Goethe, but
> proceeds beyond it to a view of poetry as a union of opposites,
> a symbol of symbols.[2]

As we consider some of the things that this "organic analogy" means,
let us begin with the most general, the concept of society. No European has better expressed the longing for a holistic society than Friedrich von Hardenberg, who, writing under his pen name Novalis, began
his essay "Christianity and Europe" (1799) with these words:

> Those were beautiful, glorious times when Europe was a
> Christian country, when *One* Christianity inhabited this part of
> the world which is formed in the image of man; *One* great
> common spiritual interest bound together the most outlying parts
> of this wide spiritual kingdom.[3]

1. H. Stuart Hughes, *Consciousness and Society,* p. 189.
2. René Wellek, *A History of Modern Criticism: 1750–1950, II, The
Romantic Age,* p. 3.
3. Novalis (Friedrich von Hardenberg), *Schriften,* I, Paul Kluckhohn and
Richard Samuel, eds., p. 507. Novalis's emphasis.

Although Novalis expressed the unity of Europe in Christian terms, and although traditional religion has considerable attraction for those who use a nonlinear paradigm, religion as such plays no inherent role in the paradigm. Society needs a unity, just as a poem does. In the twentieth century, the problem of the presence or absence of a unifying structure has been more important than its nature.

Not only does the work itself constitute a whole, as does society, but all the works taken together do so, too. To cite Wellek again:

> For [Friedrich] Schlegel literature forms "a great completely and evenly organized whole comprehending in its unity many worlds of art and itself forming a peculiar work of art." T. S. Eliot in "Tradition and the Individual Talent" has said substantially the same.[4]

We shall examine other implications of this holistic concept, and of Eliot's famous essay later.

In a holistic system, the individual art work does not exist only with reference to art; it also relates to and interacts with the world. Hence Friedrich Schelling anticipates many modernists in what Wellek characterizes as his "attempt to abolish all distinctions between art, religion, philosophy, and myth."[5] The work of art is cognitive, but not in the form of syllogistic propositions. Much modern artistic theory has interpreted art as a form of nonpropositional cognition, as August Wilhelm Schlegel did when he defined poetry as "bildlich anschauender Gedankensausdruck."[6] The nineteenth-century Russian critic Vissarion Belinsky made this virtually untranslatable phase manageable when he said, "The poet thinks in images."[7] (Of course, by quoting this famous phrase of Belinsky's, I do not imply that I share Soviet critics' belief that one can validly dissociate thought from image, and hence paraphrase a work of art as an ideological proposition.)

But the crucial figure in German thought of the romantic period is Hegel, of course, and in the "Introduction" to his *Lectures on Esthetics,* Hegel uses the traditional German distinction between *Schein* (appearance) and *Sein* (reality) in the following way:

4. Wellek, *A History of Modern Criticism: 1750–1950, II, The Romantic Age,* p. 7.
5. Ibid., p. 74.
6. Ibid., p. 42.
7. V. G. Belinsky, *Sobranie sochinenii,* F. M. Golovenchenko, ed., 1:464.

If the manner of appearance [*Erscheinungsweise*] of art forms is called illusion in comparison with the thought of philosophy, with religious and moral principles, the form of the appearance, which takes on content in the realm of thought, is in any case a true reality. Yet in comparison with the appearance of the sensuous immediate existence and with that of history, the appearance of art has the advantage that it manifests itself through itself, and indicates something spiritual which is to come to completion through it; and the immediate appearance gives itself not as illusory, but as the real and the true, while the genuine becomes contaminated and hidden by the immediate sensuous. The hard crust of nature and of the ordinary world make it more difficult for the spirit to penetrate to the Idea than for the work of art [to do so].[8]

Bergson and Nietzsche (probably unwittingly) were later to make good use of Hegel's principle that art reveals truth more completely than ordinary experience; it has proven useful in the twentieth century as well.

One does not usually associate Hegel with technology, but he did in fact first state the principle with which McLuhan shocked people a hundred and fifty years later: the interpretation of technology as the extension of man. In his *System of Philosophy: Second Part. Philosophy of Nature,* Hegel discusses contemporary science and its meaning at great length. He makes two statements in his section on "The Organic" which indicate how naturally someone who uses a holistic methodology formulates the concept of technology as the extensions of man. With regard to the binary pair organism–environment, he says:

The organism is a coming together with itself in its external process. . . .

. . . The process that enters into the external difference turns into the process of the organism itself, and the result is not the simple production [literally, "bringing out": *Hervorbringung*] of a means, but of an end—a closure with itself.[9]

If the organic makes closure with itself, one can speak of a *Bildungstrieb,* which translates roughly as "formative drive":

8. Georg Wilhelm Friedrich Hegel, *Sämtliche Werke,* Hermann Glockner, ed., 12:29–30.

9. Hegel, *Sämtliche Werke,* 9:645.

An externality which belongs to the inorganic nature of the animal becomes assimilated here: but in such a way that it remains an external object. The formative drive is like a creation from within, an externalizing of the self by the self [*ein sich selbst Äusserlich-Machen*], but as a projection [Einbildung] of the form of the organism into the external world.[10]

Naturally, I do not present these as anything more than embryonic suggestions; I have found no specific discussions of technology as the extensions of man in Hegel. Nevertheless, he stated the essence of a crucial, and still controversial, concept.

But our true concern here is not with the relationship between nineteenth- and twentieth-century thought, but with the development of the nonlinear paradigm. And if one needs a date for the beginning of this development, 1881 will serve, for in that year an elaborate experiment by the physicist Michelson disproved the theory of an "aether," an analogue that classical physics had invented for absolute space in order to explain action at a distance.[11] This experiment has great value, for it enables us to correlate the late nineteenth-century revolutions in science with those that took place in philosophy. Whether they knew of Michelson's experiment or not, Henri Bergson and Friedrich Nietzsche were the first philosophers who responded to the problems which the demise of absolute space created. They responded, furthermore, in a way that demonstrates yet again the relevance of Germany to modern culture. Although they may not have known of Michelson's experiment, they certainly knew of Kant. As Čapek puts it, "We can speak of a certain *isoformism* between the thought of Kant and Newton."[12] And since it was Kant who wished to carry through Newton's work into philosophy, the growth of the nonlinear paradigm begins with an attack on Kant.

10. Ibid., p. 661.
11. Milič Čapek, *The Philosophical Impact of Contemporary Physics,* p. 84.
12. Ibid., p. 38.

Chapter 5

The Attack on Kant

The lives, personalities, and prose styles of Henri Bergson and Friedrich Nietzsche contrast in about every way possible: the successful university professor versus the tortured outsider; the calm Frenchman versus the passionate German; the writer of limpid, understandable essays versus the creator of arresting, enigmatic aphorisms. Yet I wish to propose an intrinsic relationship between the various aspects of their work and the nonlinear paradigm, which derives from their attack on Kant, in whom they found a common enemy.

I use the word *enemy,* since in the absence of institutionalized polemic, it expresses a dichotomy. It is typical of the late nineteenth century, that its practitioners used a combination of linear and nonlinear paradigms. As both thinkers began to develop their paradigms, they began to employ dichotomies, in order to make the opposition between their work and the linear paradigm more complete. Thus, in *Creative Evolution* (1907), Bergson tells us that intelligence *"is characterized by a natural lack of comprehension of life"* (p. 635),[1] but that "Instinct is molded on the very form of life. While the intellect creates everything mechanically, instinct, so to speak, creates organically" (p. 634). In *Creative Evolution,* Bergson consistently uses the mechanical–organic or intellectual–instinctive opposition as dichotomic. Nietzsche does very much the same thing when he announces that, "The intellect is the error" (83:32),[2] and that "An instinct is weakened when it makes itself rational" (77:34).

The two also make similar statements about Kant; Bergson's

1. Page numbers after quotations from Bergson refer to the following edition: Henry Bergson, *Oeuvres.* All translations are my own, but the emphasis is Bergson's.

2. Volume and page number quotations from Nietzsche refer to the following edition: Friedrich Nietzsche, *Sämtliche Werke.* This edition appeared as part of a larger series, and I follow the publisher's practice of referring to volume 1 as volume 70, 2 as 71, and so on. All translations are my own, but the emphasis is Nietzsche's.

"Kant's error was to have taken time for a homogeneous milieu" (p. 119), implies something very much like Nietzsche's "To make assertion about the nature of things of which we know nothing was a naiveté of Kant's" (78:389). Both associate Kant with the intellect, with a belief in homogeneous time and space, and the importance which that belief attributes to sequence. Bergson says that if one thinks of time and space as having the same nature, one begins to think of time as space; it is this spatialized thought that he calls the intellect: *The more consciousness makes itself intellectual, the more matter spatializes itself*" (p. 656). Nietzsche, too, believed that concepts of time and space structure the thought patterns of modern man:

> Our senses never show us juxtaposition, but always sequence. Space and the human laws of space *assume* the reality of images, forms, and substances, and their durability; that is, our space is an imaginary world. We know nothing of space which belongs to the eternal flux of things. (83:32)

These quotations may represent a number of others, all in the same vein. Today we wish to understand Bergson and Nietzsche because of their significance in the development of the nonlinear paradigm. Although both manifested great imagination in creating ingenious and suggestive binary pairs and although they have common assumptions about the meaning of binarism, they proceed in very different ways. Let us begin with Bergson.

Bergson writes about the sensations of the "I"; ironically—and he probably did not sense the irony—he follows the Cartesian tradition of introspection that makes a dichotomy of the self and of the outer world, precisely in order to subvert that very tradition. In his first book, the *Essay on the Immediate Data of Consciousness* (1889), he examines the implications of the noncontinuous subset of the linear paradigm within his own consciousness, and finds that any belief in time as a succession of identical units destroys his sense of self. Instead, "Within me a process of mutual penetration of facts of consciousness goes on" (p. 72). Bergson posits the nature of mind, and indeed, all existence, as process; as he puts it on the first page of *Creative Evolution:*

> First of all, I assert that I pass from state to state. I am hot or cold; I am happy or I am sad; I work, or I do nothing; I look at that which surrounds me, or I think of something else.

Sensations, feelings, desires, images—here are the changes
among which my existence is divided, and which color it by
turns. I thus change unceasingly. (p. 495)

While affirming change, Bergson does not go into a dichotomy by
denying form. Memories do not lie passively in the mind, for, "One
perceives them in each other; they interpenetrate and organize themselves like the notes of a melody, by forming that which we call in
indistinct or qualitative multiplicity" (p. 70). This multiplicity forms a
binary pair past–present (we know the distinctions between them
through contrast), and gives an early affirmation of the reciprocal
relationship between structure and meaning. Furthermore, the musical
image used by Bergson insists on intrinsic historicity and the unity of
form and content.

In *Matter and Memory* (1896), Bergson presents another aspect
of the binary pair past–present as the pair memory–perception:

I meet a person for the first time: I simply perceive him. If I
meet him again. I recognize him, in the sense of the
concomitant circumstances of original perception [which] return
me to the mind, sketching around the actual image an outline
which is not the one currently perceived. To recognize thus
means to associate to a present perception images formerly in
continuity with it. (p. 236)

Or, more briefly, "Memory, inseparable in practice from perception,
interpolates the past into the present, [and] contracts into a unique
intuition the multiple moments of *durée*" (p. 219). If memory and
perception, the past and the present, interpenetrate, then we can
better understand the discussions of the role of expectations in perception.

"We are free," Bergson writes in the *Essay,* "when our acts
emanate from our entire personality, when they have that indefinable
resemblance to it which one occasionally finds between the artist and
his work" (p. 113). Thus, art implies wholeness for Bergson, who
assumes that the artist has pure perception; that is, the artist perceives
things as they are, not he remembers them. In his book *Laughter*
(1900), Bergson creates the pair artistic–ordinary perception, which
has crucial cognitive significance.

What is the object of art? If reality could strike our senses
directly, if we could enter into immediate communication with
things and with ourselves, I believe that art would be useless, or

rather that we would all be artists, since our soul would then continually vibrate in union with nature. Our eyes, aided by memory, would carve out in space and fix in time inimitable pictures. . . . Between ourselves and nature, or, better, between ourselves and our own consciousness is interposed, a veil dense for the masses of men, but thin, almost transparent, for the artist and the poet. (pp. 458–59)

We recognize here a more personal version of Hegel's statement that art "manifests itself through itself"; where Hegel abstracts, Bergson makes immediate. In any case both consider art a form of cognition.

One can relate this passage to Bergson's attack on Kant by noticing that Bergson is resolving Kant's dichotomy between the phenomenon and the neumenon. "We *can* know the neumenon," says Bergson, "and precisely in art." In esthetics, this means a resolution of the dichotomy between the work of art and the spectator who contemplates it "disinterestedly." In a nonlinear paradigm, the work of art and the spectator interact; the art work affects the perception of the spectator, whose reaction may affect the artist's subsequent works.

Bergson devotes most of *Laughter* to articulating principles that explain the technical devices he finds characteristic of the classic French comedies. He was thus examining an art form that harmonized with his esthetic theories, for comedy—and especially social satire—serves very well the purposes of the theoretician who wishes to emphasize the effect on art on the relationship between the individual and society. He begins by assuming that a society, like the psyche of an individual, exists as an integrated whole in a state of constant flux: "A previously established relationship among the people does not suffice for it [the society]; it would want a constant effort at reciprocal adaptation" (p. 396). Given this, Bergson can conclude that:

All inelasticity of character, of the spirit as well as of the body, is thus suspect for society, because it is a possible sign of an activity which isolates, which tends to divert from the common center around which society gravitates. (p. 396)

Therefore,

The comic is that side of a person in which he resembles a thing, that aspect of human events which imitates through its inelasticity of a quite special type, pure and simple mechanism, automatism, ultimately movement without life. It thus expresses an individual or collective imperfection which calls for

immediate correction. This correction is laughter. Laughter is a
certain social gesture which singles out and expresses a special
kind of distraction in men and events. (p. 428)

Although Bergson himself never says so, this inelasticity corresponds
to the spatialized thought of the linear paradigm. He thus suggests that
the binary nature of art, which springs from the, presumably, binary
perception of the artist, tends to turn linear—spatialized and intellectual—thought patterns into nonlinear ones. One finds similar implications in Nietzsche as well.

For Nietzsche, as for Bergson, laughter expresses far more than
mere amusement; it expresses the unity of the psyche (and, by implication, the unity of society as well). Many of Nietzsche's best passages
on laughter occur in *Die fröhliche Wissenschaft* (1882), or, approximately, *The Gay Science* (he refers to "gaya scienza" as a "Provencal
concept" [77:370]). Nietzsche remarks in "The Teacher of the Purpose of Existence," the first essay in *The Gay Science:*

To laugh at oneself, as one would have to laugh, in order to
laugh *from the whole truth,* the best people have not had
enough sense of truth until now, and the most gifted much too
little genius! There is perhaps still a future for laughter! . . .
Perhaps then laughter will be united with wisdom, perhaps there
will be then only a "gay science." (74:29)

Although Nietzsche would agree with Bergson that laughter corrects
rigidity in people, he would not put it that way. For Nietzsche, "art
is essentially affirmation of existence" (77:553), and laughter expresses this affirmation.

True art, for Nietzsche, as for Bergson, takes the form of drama.
While Bergson discussed the classical French theater, Nietzsche dealt
with ancient Greek tragedy, to which he devoted his first major work,
The Birth of Tragedy (1872). The work begins with an affirmation of
binarism:

We will have gained much for the study of esthetics when we
have come, not only to the logical insight, but also to the
immediate certainty, that the further development of art is tied
to the duality [*Duplicität*] of the *Apollonian* and the *Dionysian.*
(70:87)

The binary pair Apollonian–Dionysian appears not as an abstract principle, but as a way of understanding Greek—and thus Western—

cultural history. Yet such were the contradictions of late nineteenth-century thought that Nietzsche goes into a dichotomy to lament the demise of Greek tragedy, which he considers the consummate expression of binarism: "With the death of Greek tragedy there appeared an enormous emptiness, which was deeply felt everywhere" (70:102). The loss was not absolute, however, for Nietzsche later conceded that "Perhaps Provence was a high point in Europe" (82:263). Later, he argues that binarism is reappearing in Europe. Let us consider some individual issues.

It is not enough to say that the Apollonian represents reason, and the Dionysian orgiastic frenzy. When Nietzsche writes, "Apollo stands before me as the clarifying genius of the principii individuationis" (70:132), we understand that the Apollonian separates and divides; likewise, when Nietzsche refers to the chorus of Greek tragedy as "the symbol of the collected dionysically aroused masses" (70:87), we understand that the Dionysian represents that which joins or unites, especially sound or music. And this joining of centrifugal and centripetal forces created great energy in the classical age of Greek tragedy:

> And thus the double nature [*Doppelwesen*] of the Aeschylean Prometheus, his conjoint Dionysian and Apollonian nature, can be expressed in the conceptual formula: "Everything that exists is just and unjust and in both cases is equally justified." (70:97)

Binarism precludes value judgments, a fact that Nietzsche stated in his much-misunderstood formula "beyond good and evil." He argues in *The Genealogy of Morals* (1887) that the very concepts of good and evil deny binarism, and thus distort life itself. And this is why he repeatedly attacks Kant, whose philosophy he interprets as a vast structure of fixed values—especially the categorical imperative—and thus dichotomies, which preclude the dynamism of binary interaction.

Nietzsche says that Socrates, through the plays of Euripides, brought about the individuation of the Apollonian from the Dionsyian. (After all, the very questions "What is the good? What is the true?" imply static dichotomies.) As Nietzsche put it, "Here *philosophical thought* overgrows art and forces it to cling close to the trunk of dialectic. The *Apollonian* tendency has withdrawn into logical schematicism" (72:122). And at this point in the argument, the nature of imagery once again becomes important; whereas Bergson and Nietzsche both have associated the imagery of sound with binarism, at this point Nietzsche associated the dissociation of the Apollonian and the Dionysian with the eye. Possibly thinking of Polyphemus, the cyclops who tried to separate the lovers Acis and Galatea, he writes:

> Let us now think of the one large cyclops eye of Socrates turned on tragedy, that eye in which the fine frenzy of artistic inspiration has never gleamed—let us think how it was denied to that eye to look into the Dionysian abysses with pleasure— What must it have seen in the "exalted and high praised" tragic art, as Plato calls it? (70:120)

Thus, the unfeeling eye dissociates, because it cannot respond to the Dionysian; by implication, much of Western civilization, at whose beginning Socrates stands, does, too.

But this process, like all processes, has not ended. Nietzsche finds in Wagner's music, in his attempt to create a *Gesamtkunstwerk,* a rebirth of tragedy, i.e., of binarism. In Wagner's music, "Dionysus speaks the language of Apollo; Apollo finally [speaks] that of Dionysus; thereby the highest goal of tragedy and art in general is reached" (70:173). It is this statement, we realize, which has made all the others possible. Concerned with binarism as he was, Nietzsche could not have perceived the linear paradigm as he did without believing that the age in which he lived was beginning to break with it.

Since Nietzsche understood Western culture as an overemphasis on the Apollonian, he stresses the artistic and the philosophical potential of the Dionysian all the more. When he wants to adopt Hegel for his own purposes to say that sufficiently Dionysian art helps people to understand the universe, he has recourse to the same image as Bergson, the image of removing a veil.

> In the Dionysian dithyramb man is raised to the highest pitch of all his symbolic capacities; something never before experienced demands an outlet, the annihilation of the veil of Maya, oneness as the genius of nature, yes, of nature. (70:56)

If art shows us true reality, a reality that ordinary people do not perceive, the artist's perception must somehow differ from that of ordinary people. Nietzsche gives this difference far more attention than does Bergson, and in a particularly enigmatic way at that.

In his challenging fashion, Nietzsche announces that, "It does not seem possible to be an artist, and not to be sick" (78:545). This statement only seems to contradict "Art is essentially affirmation of existence," for the sickness of the artist consists in recognizing the dichotomies of his society. If "The innocence of becoming gives us the greatest freedom" (78:530), and if becoming consists in the interchange between the Apollonian and the Dionysian, then dichotomies block this interchange, and create sickness. Such is Nietzsche's argument in *The Genealogy of Morals,* where ideals, or fixed values, create the dichotomy good–bad, and its consequent weaknesses.

If the Apollonian and the Dionysian coexist in the artist, and if art annihilates the veil of Maya, then this binary nature of art appears in other ways as well. Although art and nature interact, they are not the same in any literal way. Nietzsche makes the point in his usual striking way by comparing the artist to a liar: "The poet sees in the liar his sibling [*Milchbruder*], whose milk he has taken away" (74:169). By this comparison, Nietzsche is emphasizing the falseness, that is to say, the artifice of art. In a binary system, that which reveals truth is itself untruthful, i.e., unnatural.

Thus, Bergson and Nietzsche make closely analogous arguments about the nature of binarism. Since they lived in a transitional age, they also thought a good deal about the difference between binary pairs and dichotomies (which they construed as a difference between sequence and juxtaposition), and the creation of dichotomies. For both of them, the withdrawal from shared experience creates dichotomies, and they both use examples from the theater to make the point. For Bergson, rigidity of personality means a withdrawal from society, which the laughter of art corrects; for Nietzsche, who had a more historical mind, the demise of the chorus signaled what he called the splitting off (individuation) of the Apollonian and the Dionysian. Bergson thought of dichotomies primarily with regard to time; for him, dichotomies spatialize thought and make it impossible to think of change that preserves unity. *Continuity* means for Bergson very much what *becoming* means for Nietzsche, who interpreted the dichotomies of his own time as resulting from fixed values, which he called ideals, and value judgments such as good–bad.

Nietzsche's emphasis on the demise of the chorus in Greek tragedy reminds us that when Bergson and Nietzsche affirmed binarism, they both associated it not only with laughter, but also with music. Both associations imply a concept of sound as a process that occurs between a speaker and a hearer. Denial of this process means a denial of the interaction with other humans, and this, naturally, creates a dichotomy. When he needs an image to express this process, Nietzsche chooses the eye.

One can readily distinguish this cyclops eye, which individuates, from the visual images which Bergson and Nietzsche use to express the means by which art reveals reality. Although neither discusses the matter in detail (one has the impression that they felt a need to deal with less complex matters first), they surely had in mind something like poetic vision, as opposed to the physiological ability to see.

Finally, one should note that the association of art and philosophy found a natural expression in the work of thinkers like Bergson and Nietzsche, who themselves possessed considerable literary gifts. This combination of thinker and artist proved particularly creative among the modernists, who generalized the attack on Kant to include the Renaissance.

Chapter 6

The Attack on the Renaissance

In this chapter, I propose to show how modernist writers and thinkers developed and applied the nonlinear principles that Bergson and Nietzsche had articulated. Of necessity, I will be dealing with a small but distinguished group of practitioners (primarily Wilhelm Worringer, T. E. Hulme, T. S. Eliot, and Ezra Pound) and one which has substantial affinities with other groups. A detailed comparison with Russian futurism and Russian formalist theory, for example, would suggest close similarities, and by making allowance for differences in cultural tradition, one could find analogous statements in the works of various French, German, and Italian modernists.

It will prove essential here to deal with the modernists as though they were informants in the linguistic sense. I do not propose to ask whether their statements are right or wrong, but whether they are coherent. Furthermore, since the twentieth century has given rise to a plethora of theoretical statements, terminology has accordingly proliferated. It may simplify analysis to reinterpret positions in terms of the linear and nonlinear paradigms.

Given the relevance of German culture to the nonlinear paradigm, it seems appropriate to begin with a German theorist, Wilhelm Worringer, whose book *Abstraction and Empathy* (1908) enjoyed great popularity. Worringer knew his Nietzsche and Bergson, as well as art historians such as Theodor Lipps and Alois Riegl. We may consider him the thinker who began combining various aspects of the nonlinear paradigm. In his book (his dissertation, actually), he sets up abstraction and empathy as another of the oppositions that characterize twentieth-century thought. Like many others, Worringer sometimes treats the components as a binary pair, and sometimes as a dichotomy.

Essentially, Worringer wishes to replace the concept of art history as a linear progression that reaches a peak in the art of the Renaissance with an explicitly binary theory that has no value judgments:

> We must first have grasped the phenomenon of classical art in
> its deepest essence in order to recognize that classicism means
> nothing complete and closed, but [is] only one pole in the
> circling orbit of the artistic process. The evolutionary history of
> art is as round as the universe, and no pole exists which does
> not have its counter-pole.[1]

The point, of course, is that representational art had for centuries
enjoyed the stature of a privileged frame of reference, in comparison
with which one could judge all art. Yet here the recurring irony appears: precisely because representational art had the inertia of prestige, Worringer could not simply change from linear to nonlinear
thought, and went into a dichotomy himself by reversing the earlier
value judgment.

> With Gothic, the last style disappears. Whoever has felt in some
> degree all that lies in this unnaturalness will, for all his joy at the
> new possibilities which the Renaissance created, remain
> conscious with deep regret of the values consecrated by a great
> tradition which were lost forever with this victory of the organic
> and the natural.[2]

In lamenting the demise of the Middle Ages, Worringer begins the
elegiac strain that characterizes most modernist historical thought
(and that also reminds us of Novalis). As modernists began to use
binary pairs, they had an intense awareness of the meaning of binarism in other societies.

The binary pair art–nature makes it possible to establish a relationship between the thought patterns of a society and the art that
arises in that society. Worringer takes up Alois Riegl's concept of
Kunstwollen, or "will to art," and defines it as "that latent inner drive
to understand, which, quite independently of the object and the
means of creation, exists for itself and which behaves as the will to
form."[3] This will to art, actually a special case of metaphors for energy
such as Nietzsche's "will to power" and Bergson's *élan vital,* manifests itself in two different forms:

> As the urge to empathy as a pre-assumption of esthetic
> experience finds its gratification in the beauty of the organic, so
> the urge to abstraction finds its beauty in the life-denying

1. Wilhelm Worringer, *Abstraction und Einfühlung,* p. 172.
2. Ibid., pp. 164–65.
3. Ibid., p. 42.

inorganic, in the crystalline, or, speaking generally, in all abstract regularity and necessity.[4]

Not content to make this distinction, and use it to discuss art, he makes the following vital connection:

> The style most perfect in its regularity, the style of the highest abstraction and the strictest exclusion of [the representation of] life is peculiar to peoples at the most primitive levels of culture. Therefore there must exist a causal relationship between primitive culture and the highest, purest regular art form. And further, the proposition may be stated: the less mankind, by virtue of its spiritual knowledge, has made friends with the appearance of the external world and has achieved a relationship of trust to it, the more powerful is the dynamic from which that highest abstract beauty will be striven for.
>
> It is not that the primitive man sought regularity in nature more urgently, or experienced regularity in it more intensely, quite the opposite: because he stands so lost and spiritually helpless amid the things of the external world, because he experiences only a lack of clarity, and an arbitrariness in his relationship to, and the interplay of, the things of the external world, is the urge so intense in him to take from the things of the external world their lack of clarity and arbitrariness, [and] to give them a value of necessity and a value of regularity.[5]

In relating abstraction and empathy to unconscious psychological attitudes, Worringer is assuming that a society creates art with a composition that contrasts with the nature of the paradigm it has internalized. Binarism, when applied to perception, implies that we perceive most intensely when we perceive by contrast. Thus, societies that have internalized a nonlinear paradigm, create an art in which lines predominate—a "geometric style" (Riegl's term) that seems "perfect in its regularity"; societies that have internalized a linear paradigm create an art in which the sinuous, flowing curves of the organic predominate. Clearly, he is saying that empathy appears in societies with technologies that protect them from the threat of animals and natural phenomena; societies so protected can find beauty in organic forms and attempt exact imitations of those forms in their art. Societies that lack such technology exist largely at the mercy of the natural environment and thus create a geometric style that mediates between

4. Ibid., p. 36.
5. Ibid., pp. 51–52.

them and nature. Such reasoning implies the concept of society that Bergson used in *Laughter*—the concept that a society exists as a dynamic, interrelated whole, and that it reacts to stress in order to re-establish this internal organization.

While Worringer resembles Bergson and Nietzsche in assuming that art has a vital function in the society as a whole, he was too impressed with Riegl's studies of Egyptian art and too entranced with Gothic architecture, to share Nietzsche's awareness of what modern art implies about society. (Worringer had probably seen very little Postimpressionist art.) But one outspoken Englishman had read Nietzsche, Bergson, and Worringer, and had seen some modern art, too; that was T. E. Hulme.

Hulme, who because he died in World War I in 1917 had a relatively brief career, has a seminal importance in the development of the nonlinear paradigm. By about 1914, he had set forth several of its essential principles. Whereas Worringer uses the binary pair society–environment almost exclusively, Hulme adds to it the pair individual–society, which he uses analogously. Here Hulme is continuing Bergson's concern with the immediate data of consciousness in order to enrich what Worringer had done. Whereas Worringer theorizes only about the past, Hulme does what neither Bergson nor Worringer thought of doing: he applies all the theory he knows in an impassioned attempt to understand the nature of the present.

Hulme had an intuitive understanding of Bergson's principle that perception operates as a circuit. He anticipates Kuhn when he says, "You have in your mind a model of what is clear and comprehensible, and the process of explanation consists in explaining all the phenomena of nature in the terms of this model."[6] Hulme also anticipated Kuhn's concern with changes in paradigms. With regard to the meaning of change in art styles, he declares, "To see this is a kind of conversion. It radically alters our physical perception; so that the world takes on an entirely different aspect."[7] Assuming the paradigmatic nature of perception, he concludes, "The ultimate reality is a circle of persons, *i.e.,* animals who communicate."[8] If we recall here Kuhn's first chapter, "A Role for History," we understand the Bergsonian nature of Hulme's statement—the first of many, incidentally, that will use the circle as an image for the nonlinear paradigm. Human

6. T. E. Hulme, *Speculations,* p. 176.
7. Ibid., p. 71.
8. Ibid., p. 217. Hulme's emphasis.

beings, Hulme's "animals who communicate," can do so because each has internalized the same paradigm (a process that occurred in the past), and uses that paradigm to create the present. By definition, then, no one individual discovers experience for himself, and dichotomies are an illusion. Cognition occurs as an interactive process, an interchange between individual and environment.

Hulme takes this understanding of cognition, and combines it with the tripartite historical scheme of *The Birth of Tragedy,* which —as the major text on nonlinear historical development—proved paradigmatic for modernists in general. There results, not merely a principle, but the first genuine interpretation of modern art (Hulme thinks primarily of his friend Henri Gaudier-Brzeska) as nonpropositional cognition.

> If the argument I have followed is correct, I stand committed to two statements:—(1) . . . that a new geometrical art is emerging which may be considered as different in kind from the art which preceded it, it being much more akin to the geometrical arts of the past, and (2) . . . that this change from a vital to a geometrical art is the product of and will be accompanied by a certain change of sensibility, a certain change of general attitude, and that this new attitude will differ in kind from the humanism which has prevailed from the Renaissance to now, and will have certain analogies to the attitude of which geometrical art was the expression in the past.[9]

Here the terminology begins to accumulate. Hulme's "geometric" and "vital" art corresponds to Worringer's "abstraction" and "empathy," of course. More important, Hulme is applying to the visual arts the scheme that Nietzsche applied to music and tragedy. The new geometrical art is akin to the geometrical arts of the past, as Wagner's operas are akin to classical Greek tragedies. The "general attitude which has prevailed from the Renaissance to now" corresponds to post-Socratic thought that "individuated" the Apollonian from the Dionysian. In the phrase "change of sensibility," we find a synthesis of Nietzsche, Bergson, and Worringer in the correlation of artistic change and individual perception.

In these comments, Hulme is taking the binary pair past–present more seriously and is using it more consistently than Bergson himself. In his statements on the cognitive significance of art in *Laughter,*

9. Ibid., p. 91.

Bergson attributes no temporal quality to the reality art reveals. He denies (implicitly, anyhow) his own emphasis on the principle that everything exists as flux. Hulme has renounced the traditional generalities of philosophical discourse for a concern with the immediate data of consciousness. In so doing, he has affirmed an essential implication of the binary pair past–present, namely that history, as an individual experiences it, has coherence. Since various historical periods interpenetrate (as Bergson would have put it), sequence alone offers an inadequate explanation of social and artistic change. The present thus has greater affinities with some periods of the past than with others.

Modernists rarely made any serious, long-term attempts to apply the principle that art gives cognition, at least with regard to specific works, but they often affirmed it—primarily as a means of distinguishing themselves from the cliché of "art for art's sake." Hulme puts the matter very tentatively: "May not the change of sensibility, in a region like aesthetics, a by-path in which we are, as it were, off our guard, some indication that the *humanist tradition is breaking up*—for individuals here and there, at any rate?"[10] Eliot, who felt a close kinship with Hulme, emphasized the binary pair individual–society and made general applications of the principle to his favorite poets of the past in "Shakespeare and the Stoicism of Seneca" (1927):

> The great poet, in writing himself, writes his time. Thus Dante, hardly knowing it, became the voice of the thirteenth century; Shakespeare, hardly knowing it, became the representative of the end of the sixteenth century, of a turning point in history.[11]

What Eliot does not say in his magisterial prose is often as important as what he does say; and here he is clearly thinking of Hulme's argument that modern art (in this case, poetry) means "the breakup of the humanist tradition."

Ezra Pound's essays have a ring of American colloquialism that distinguishes them from those of Hulme and Eliot, but he expresses similar attitudes. Pound can state the cognitive significance of art very simply, as when he says in "The Serious Artist" (1913) that "Bad art is inaccurate art. It is art that makes false reports."[12] He tells us the subject of art's reports in "The Teacher's Mission" (1934) in lines that

10. Ibid., p. 55. Hulme's emphasis.
11. T. S. Eliot, *Selected Essays,* p. 117.
12. Ezra Pound, *Literary Essays of Ezra Pound,* p. 43.

indicate something of what he learned from the futurists: "A nation's writers are the voltometers and steam-gauges of that nation's intellectual life."[13] Because Wyndham Lewis worked both as a writer and as an artist, his statements present unusual interest; he articulates the concept of art as knowledge of society more completely than Pound, and gives an example. The following passage occurs in *Time and Western Man* (1928):

> If you want to know what is actually occurring inside, underneath, at the centre, at any given moment, art is a truer guide than "politics," more often than not. Its movements represent, in an acute form, a deeper emotional truth, although not discursively. *The Brothers Karamazov,* for example, is a more cogent document for the history of its period than any record of actual events.[14]

From the generative statements of the philosophers, and then the artists, the concept that art presents a form of nonpropositional cognition about the society in which it arises gradually achieved the status of a consensus in the twentieth century and thus acquired validity among theorists of many different kinds. Although this aspect of the growth of the nonlinear paradigm deserves detailed attention, it must suffice here to indicate the generality of the paradigm by quoting a statement made by J. L. Fisher, an anthropologist, in 1961.

> It is assumed that the artist is in some sense keenly aware of the social structure and model personality of his culture, although of course he cannot necessarily or usually put his awareness into social science jargon or even into common-sense words.[15]

One could cite numerous statements to the same effect, but they all share a certain abstract quality. Virtually no one before McLuhan consistently applied the principle in question to various kinds of art works in various periods.

If art serves as cognition, the society creates an interchange by reacting to that cognition. All the artists and thinkers I have quoted in this and the previous chapter have believed that the cognitive quality of art implies its functional nature in society, but none of them had more intimate knowledge of the modernist change of sensibility (what

13. Ibid., p. 58.
14. Wyndham Lewis, *Time and Western Man,* p. 120.
15. J. L. Fisher, "Art Styles as Cultural Cognitive Maps," p. 80.

Kuhn calls the "gestalt switch"), and none expressed it more clearly than did Pablo Picasso, who once told Françoise Gilot the following story:

> When I became interested, forty years ago, in Negro Art and I made what they refer to as the Negro period in my painting, it was because at that time I was against what was called beauty in the museums. At that time, for most people a Negro mask was an ethnographic object. When I went for the first time, at Derain's urging, to the Trocadero museum, the smell of dampness and rot there stuck in my throat. It depressed me so much that I wanted to get out fast, but I stayed and studied. Men had made those masks and other objects for a sacred purpose, as a kind of mediation between themselves and the unknown hostile forces that surrounded them, in order to overcome their fear and horror by giving it form and image. At that moment I realized that this was what painting was all about. Painting isn't an aesthetic operation; it's a form of magic designed as a mediator between this strange, hostile world and us, a way of seizing the power of giving form to our terrors as well as our desires. When I came to that realization, I knew I had found my way.[16]

Picasso so closely agrees with Worringer here that one suspects he had been reading his work. Picasso certainly does not represent an age that, as Worringer put it, "made friends with the appearance of the external world." Picasso and Worringer associate geometrical form, a psychosocial function for art, and religion.

This cluster of associations appeared in modernist interest in primitive poetry as well as in primitive painting and sculpture. While one might think that Eliot, for example, would have taken little interest in primitive art, he wrote about it very much as Hulme had, in "War Paint and Feathers" (1919), a review of a volume of American Indian songs and chants:

> And as it is certain that some study of primitive man furthers our understanding of civilized man, so it is certain that primitive art and poetry help our understanding of civilized art and poetry. . . .
> . . . He [the artist] is the most ready and the most able of men to learn from the savage; he is the first man to perceive that there are aspects in which the lays of the Dimbovitza or

16. Françoise Gilot, *Life With Picasso*, p. 266.

the Arapajos are a more profitable study and a more dignified performance, than "Aurora Leigh" and "Kehama."

He will welcome the publication of primitive poetry because it has more significance in relation to its own age or culture than "Kehama" and "Aurora Leigh" have for theirs.[17]

Obviously, art can have a cognitive function only if it has "significance in relation to its own age or culture," and modernists found in primitive art that inherent relationship to society which they wished their own art to have.

Our discussion of paradigms and the manner in which primitive art embodies them creates a context in which we can understand the modernist attitude toward the Middle Ages; a key to this approach is the often-misunderstood word *impersonal*. Eliot states, for example, "The emotion of art is impersonal."[18] *Impersonal* here means, not something like "untouched by human hands," which suggests a dichotomy, but "suprapersonal," shared, communal, and—above all—*paradigmatic*. Hence, Eliot can define "the advantages of a coherent traditional system of dogma and morals like the Catholic" in the following way: "It stands apart, for understanding and assent even without belief, from the single individual who propounds it."[19] This application of paradigms to religion explains the appeal of Roman Catholicism for Hulme, Eliot, and even Joyce (as well as McLuhan). If perception and art have a paradigmatic nature, great art requires a great, socially institutionalized paradigm: hence the often repeated modernist admiration for Dante, whose work expresses such a paradigm and presents a verbal analogy to the Gothic architecture that Worringer (and other modernists) admired so fervently.

A harmony of attitude about the paradigmatic nature of communication existed with Hulme and Eliot, on one hand, and with Pound on the other, as the following statement by Pound suggests: "It is tremendously important that great poetry be written, it makes no jot of difference who writes it."[20] A man of more varied tastes than Hulme or Eliot, Pound especially admired the poetry of Provence and China. An explanation of the nature of his admiration for Chinese

17. T. S. Eliot, "Review of *The Path of the Rainbow: An Anthology of Songs and Chants from the Indians of North America,* ed. George W. Cronyn."

18. Eliot, "Tradition and the Individual Talent," in *Selected Essays,* p. 11.

19. Eliot, "Dante," in *Selected Essays,* p. 219.

20. Pound, "A Retrospect," in *Essays,* p. 10.

poetry involves an analysis of ideograms, but Provençal poetry, as a part of Western tradition, offers fewer conceptual difficulties.

"Any study of European poetry is unsound if it does not commence with a study of that art in Provence."[21] In such assertions, Pound is (probably unconsciously) continuing Nietzsche's in a number of respects. We recall, for example, Nietzsche's comment that the "gaya scienza" was a "Provençal concept," and that "Perhaps Provence was a high point of Europe." Furthermore, Pound has a very Nietzschean insistence on the role of music in organizing poetry.

> It is not intelligent to ignore the fact that both in Greece and in Provence the poetry attained its highest rhythmic and metrical brilliance at times when the arts of verse and music were most closely knit together, when each thing done by the poet had some definite musical urge or necessity bound up within it.[22]

Or as Pound puts it with regard to a Provençal poet whom he particularly admires: "And the art of En Ar. Daniel is not literature but the art of fitting words well with music, wellnigh a lost art."[23] And, as with the Greek tragedy Nietzsche refers to, Provençal poetry combines the qualities of artificiality, sound, and public performance, and it is virtually the only European poetry that does: "The forms of this poetry are highly artificial. . . . If you wish to make love to women in public, and out loud, you must resort to subterfuge."[24] For Pound, Provençal poetry was an immediacy, not an antiquarian's delight. The relationship between his insistence on the importance of the merger of music and poetry in Provence and his own poetics emerges clearly from the following quotation:

> No one is so foolish as to suppose that a musician using "four-four" time is compelled to use always four quarter notes in each bar, or in "seven-eighths" time to use seven eighth notes uniformly in each bar. He may use one ½, one ¼, and one ⅛ rest, or any such combination as he may happen to choose or find fitting.
> To apply this musical truism to verse is to employ *vers libre.*[25]

21. Pound, "Troubadours—Their Sorts and Conditions," ibid., p. 101.
22. Pound, "The Tradition," ibid., p. 91.
23. Pound, "Arnaut Daniel," ibid., p. 112.
24. Pound, "Troubadours," ibid., p. 94.
25. Pound, "The Tradition," ibid., p. 93.

Nietzsche would have said that Pound wanted the Dionysian qualities of music to structure his work, as it did that of the poets of Provence.

But Provençal poetry, like classical tragedy, experienced the individuation of the Apollonian and the Dionysian, and Pound associated this individuation with literacy, which denies the public nature of art: "When men began to write on tablets and ceased singing to the *barbitos,* a loss of some sort was unavoidable."[26] This "loss" was the Renaissance.

Developing Worringer's ideas on the Renaissance, Hulme said that the "change of sensibility" which created modernism

> . . . has made us realize that what we took to be the necessary principles of aesthetic, constitute in reality only a psychology of Renaissance and Classical Art. At the same time, it has made us realize the essential *unity* of these latter arts. For we see that they both rest on certain common pre-suppositions, of which we only become conscious when we see them *denied* by other arts. . . . In the same way an understanding of the religious philosophy which preceded the Renaissance makes the essential unity of all philosophy since seem at once obvious.[27]

If one thinks in terms of contrasting paradigms, as the modernists did, then the differences in the *use* of a single paradigm make very little difference. Hulme knew far too much to suggest that no differences existed between, say, Descartes and John Stuart Mill. Had he read Chomsky, though, he would have said that the differences refer to surface structure, while the similarity appears in deep structure.

Thus, the binary quality of twentieth-century thought and art associates it with the Middle Ages on one hand, and with primitive civilization on the other; all three groups of cultures form a unity that differs from post-Renaissance culture, or "humanism," which is characterized by dichotomies. Once again, the pervasive irony occurs that modernists went into a dichotomy (past–present) about dichotomies, as Eliot does in this passage after referring to *Speculations:*

> I agree with what Hulme says; and I am afraid that many modern Humanists are explicitly or implicitly committed to the view which Hulme denounces; and that they are, in

26. Pound, "Troubadours," ibid., p. 101.
27. Hulme, *Speculations,* pp. 12–13. Hulme's emphasis.

consequence, men of the Renaissance rather than men of our own time.[28]

The dichotomy that most concerns Hulme is art–religion. In a memorable comment that sums up much of modernist sensibility, he said: "At the Renaissance, there were many pictures with religious subjects, but no religious art in the proper sense of the word."[29] Religious art "in the proper sense of the word" has a social function, and creates cognition by using an institutionalized paradigm. One cannot make such statements about the assertion of individualism in the Renaissance. Such reasoning produces all the modernists' judgments of the Renaissance, even when these judgments refer only to artistic quality, as Pound does when he says that after the great period of Provence passed, "The literature of the Mediterranean races continued in a steady descending curve of renaissance-ism."[30] The British art historian Clive Bell made a similar statement about painting: "More first-rate art was produced in Europe between the years 500 and 900 than was produced in the same countries between 1450 and 1850."[31] Possibly the most explicit, and most personal, statement on the issue comes from Hans Arp:

> The Renaissance taught men the haughty exaltation of their reason. Modern times, with science and technology, turned men towards megalomania. The confusion of our epoch results from this over-estimation of reason. We [Dadaists] wanted an anonymous and collective art.[32]

Naturally, the attack on the Renaissance involved more than just the Renaissance—it involved all art that shared the presuppositions of the period. Various artists and theorists took up Nietzsche's attack on Greek art after the "individuation" of the Apollonian from the Dionysian. One thinks of such well-known examples as the Italian futurists' attack on the nude in sculpture and painting, and Bertholt Brecht's attacks on Aristotelian conventions in the theater.

The romantics, as heirs of the Renaissance, came in for their share of abuse, too; Hulme provides my favorite example:

28. Eliot, "Second Thoughts on Humanism," *Selected Essays,* p. 437.

29. Hulme, *Speculations,* p. 9.

30. Pound, "Cavalcanti"; first published, 1934, p. 192.

31. Clive Bell, *Art,* p. 101. Cf. Michael Holroyd's statement that Bell's friend Roger Fry "had once declared that the Old Masters made him sick." Michael Holroyd, *Lytton Strachey,* 2:87.

32. Hans (Jean) Arp, *On My Way: Poetry and Essays, 1912–1947,* p. 40.

I object even to the best of the romantics. I object still more to the receptive attitude. I object to the sloppiness which doesn't consider that a poem is a poem unless it is moaning or whining about something or other.[33]

In his forthright way, Hulme is objecting to the assumption that true poetry consists of vaporous effusions over spring flowers and lost love —in short that true poetry uses the dichotomy self–society. In "Dante" (1929), Eliot adopts a more urbane tone, and makes the dichotomy, as well as his objection to it, more explicit: "With Goethe . . . I often feel too acutely 'this is what Goethe the man believed,' instead of merely entering into a world which Goethe has created."[34] For modernists, great poetry requires a great paradigm, and Eliot, who remained insensitive to Goethe's classicism, failed to find such a paradigm in Goethe's work. As for Pound, he hardly mentioned the romantics. His silence speaks loudly.

Although modernists attacked the romantics with great enthusiasm, they waged a better-known polemic against Milton. In "The Renaissance" (1914), Pound put it with his usual bluntness: "Milton is the worst sort of poison. He is a thorough-going decadent in the worst sense of the term."[35] Eliot's more famous statement in "The Metaphysical Poets" (1921) introduces a term for the creation of dichotomies: "In the seventeenth century a dissociation of sensibility set in, from which we have never recovered; and this dissociation, as is natural, was aggravated by the influence of the two most powerful poets of the century, Milton and Dryden."[36] We recognize a familiar theme here: the dissociation of thinking and feeling, another term for Nietzsche's individuation of the Apollonian and the Dionysian. Eliot laments the creation of the dichotomy as much as Nietzsche did, or as much as Worringer in his comments on the demise of Gothic architecture. I do not wish to lament the dichotomy; the time for lamentations has passed. I wish to understand the implications of the dichotomy, and Marjorie Hope Nicolson's book *The Breaking of the Circle* helps to do just this.

The Breaking of the Circle has great theoretical importance, for it deals with the relationship between poetry and science in the age of Donne and Shakespeare, the age with which the modernists felt an

33. Hulme, *Speculations,* p. 126.
34. Eliot, *Selected Essays,* p. 219.
35. Pound, *Selected Essays,* p. 216.
36. Eliot, *Selected Essays,* p. 247.

affinity. Essentially, the book describes the process by means of which the linear paradigm replaced the nonlinear paradigm. Nicolson begins by associating the circle with the nonlinear paradigm, in the same manner as Hulme would have.

> The cosmology of the Renaissance poets . . . was most often interpreted in terms of the circle—a circle that existed in the perfect spheres of the planets, in the circular globe, in the round head of man. This was not mere analogy to them; it was truth.[37]

But this truth, or paradigm, ended, and Nicolson shows why, in her discussion of a number of fields of science, such as medicine and astronomy. I adduce here two crucial passages, and draw the reader's attention to the individuating quality of the eye—familiar to us from Nietzsche—in the first passage, and the spatialized images of the second.

> In more senses than one Galileo had seen through heaven and found no Heavenly City, but instead "stars innumerable" never seen by human eye, the true nature of the Milky Way, a new moon, possibly a new world in that moon, and four new "planets," which though they proved not planets but satellites of Jupiter, were to be as effectual as new planets in destroying not only the old astronomy but—what mattered more to man— the very basis of the old astronomy.[38]

> The position of the earth had changed. The heavens no longer declared external and immutable values. Gone was Nature's nest of concentric boxes, evidence of permanence and stability, gone even more the supreme proof of limitation—the limits of the universe.[39]

Correlating these statements, and some others like them, with modernist theory, will prove a means of relating the themes of this chapter to one another.

Given the general distaste for Milton among British modernists, we learn with some interest from Nicolson that, "In the astronomy of

37. Marjorie Hope Nicolson, *The Breaking of the Circle*, p. 7. Cf. Worringer: "The Egyptian, we must conclude, saw, for example, in the circle, not the living line . . . but he saw in it only the geometrical form which presented itself as the most complete, in that it alone continuously fulfills the postulate of symmetry on all sides" (*Abstraction und Einfühlung*, p. 106).

38. Nicolson, *Breaking of the Circle*, p. 119.

39. Ibid., p. 167.

Paradise Lost, Milton, whether or not he realized it, broke the Circle of Perfection.''[40] That is to say, Milton's poetry represents the replacement of the nonlinear by the linear paradigm. For Hulme, Eliot, and Pound, Milton thus played a role in English poetry analogous to the role which Euripides played in Greek tragedy for Nietzsche. Now Nietzsche associated Euripides with Socrates, and Nicolson offers a thinker whom we can associate with Milton.

> The Miltonic influence was very important; yet there was a different attitude complementing, and in the hands of lesser poets, distorting the Miltonic tradition. To understand the full radiance of the light which shines in so much eighteenth-century poetry, we must add to the influence of Milton that of Newton.[41]

If Milton broke the Circle of Perfection, and if the same isoformism exists between Milton and Newton as between Kant and Newton, we can understand Eliot's and Pound's attacks on Milton as the poets' counterparts to the philosophers' attack on Kant. In both cases, what is really at stake is the linear paradigm, and not the work of a particular individual.

We have analyzed the development of the nonlinear paradigm after the first statements of its principles by Bergson and Nietzsche. While retaining essential agreement on the paradigmatic nature of cognition, on the nature of art, and thus on the social function of art, the poets made the first applications of nonlinear principles to specific artists and historical periods. In so doing, they articulated a provocative understanding of Western cultural history. Denying that change means progress, modernists asserted that the Renaissance, the great change in Western culture, meant retrogression because it broke medieval binary pairs into dichotomies. They wished to create binary theory, and thus felt an affinity with medieval and primitive cultures, in which they found socially institutionalized binarism.

The analogies between modernist theory and the interpretation of Western culture in *Understanding Media* are obvious, of course, particularly in Pound's emphasis on the meaning of sound, and on the significance of written composition as opposed to oral performance. I have refrained from dwelling on these analogies because of the absence of a vital topic in the poets' essays: technology. We cannot

40. Ibid., p. 186.
41. Marjorie Hope Nicolson, *Newton Demands the Muse,* p. 4.

discuss McLuhan's work—which is to say, we cannot address such questions as "How and why did the dissociation of sensibility occur?" —before finding the forerunners whose statements validate the principle that technology functions as the extension of man.

Chapter 7

Technology as the Extension of Man

Theories of art and culture in the twentieth century have benefited greatly from the unity of theorist and practitioner in a single person. This pattern does not appear in theories of technology in the twentieth century, for—with the possible exception of Buckminster Fuller—theorist and practitioner have not united, or even communicated. Most people who have bothered to write about modern technology have used a linear paradigm either to praise it for the progress it will inevitably bring, or to attack it as destructive. Americans frequently encounter the first attitude, and thus it needs no illustration. Jacques Ellul offers an extreme statement of the second one when he writes, "Technology encompasses the totality of present-day society. Man is caught like a fly in a bottle. His attempts at culture, freedom, and creative endeavor have become mere entities in technique's filing cabinet."[1] This chapter will analyze a group of writers who use neither half of the dichotomy free will–determinism. Rather, they derive the principle that technology functions as the extension of man from the binary pair organism–environment.

It might seem that the writers to be considered here have little in common besides their interest in a particular concept of technology. We will begin with Ernst Kapp, an obscure nineteenth-century German, and then take up Bergson, Ernst Cassirer, the Swiss scholar Jean Gebser, the paleontologist-theologian Pierre Teilhard de Chardin, S.J., and conclude with the American architectural historian Lewis Mumford. Despite the variety of cultural backgrounds and professional interests that separate these men, they have certain common assumptions. They think in holistic terms, and thus refuse to let any one subject restrict their interests. Furthermore, technology—no matter how one defines it—implies change, and thus these writers usually consider the appearance of technology among primitive (nonliterate) peoples, where change becomes particularly obvious. And, finally,

1. Jacques Ellul, *The Technological Society,* p. 417.

everyone insists on the effect of technology on those who create and use it.

Given the relevance of German culture to the rise of nonlinear paradigm, it is appropriate to begin this chapter with Ernst Kapp, whose book *Outlines of a Philosophy of Technology* (1877) is the first work that states and develops the hypothesis that technology functions as the extension of man. Kapp's long career began with the publication in 1845 of his *Philosophical or Comparative General Geography,* which he reissued in a much-revised version in 1868. The second edition expresses his new awareness of technology—especially the railroad and the telegraph—which he acquired during a long stay in the United States. It contains, in addition to systematic essays on the geographic regions of the world, Kapp's prescient attempts to interpret history and politics in terms of technology,[2] and his statements of forms of technology as sign systems, such as: "Every new industrial invention is, insofar as it becomes common property through the speed of communication, an announcement from one people to another."[3] Again and again he strikes a prophetic note when he suggests that technology will bring about a united world: "Inventions are a very distinct language; in them culminates mankind's striving to make of the planet a realm of beauty and the spirit."[4]

Unlike *General Comparative Geography, Outlines of a Philosophy of Technology* does not resemble a textbook. Nevertheless, it does have a pragmatic rather than a theoretical character, despite a number of quotations from Hegel. In an introductory chapter, Kapp states some principles of technology that other writers on the subject will echo. He declares, for example, that "Psychology and physiology have been foreign to each other long enough"[5] and believes that a crucial fact about media is "the unconscious effect."[6] Thus, "Objects of consciousness return to man's interiority . . . and they become part of interiority."[7] If perception forms a circuit, as Kapp—following Hegel and anticipating Bergson—is arguing here, and if people

2. See, for example, Kapp's analysis of Napoleon's use of communication; Ernst Kapp, *Vergleichende allgemeine Erdkunde in wissenschaftlicher Darstellung,* pp. 659ff.

3. Ibid., p. 673.

4. Ibid.

5. Ernst Kapp, *Grundlinien einer Philosophie der Technik,* p. 5.

6. Ibid., p. 141.

7. Ibid., p. 23.

now live in a world of technological devices, it logically follows that:

> From the first crude tool adapted to increase the power and dexterity of the hand in joining and separating material substances, to the most highly developed "System of Requirements" as displayed at a world exhibition, man sees and recognizes in all these exterior objects (in distinction from unaltered objects of nature), the creation of man's hand, deeds of man's spirit, the unconsciously finding, unconsciously inventing man—himself. Taking up an assumption of this sort for the totality of the field which embraces cultural objects of the external world is an actual avowal of human nature and becomes, through the act of returning the copy from the exterior to the interior, self-recognition.
>
> This occurs because for man the precedents and laws of his unconscious life come to consciousness in the use and comparative observation of the works of his hand through a genuine manifestation of the self. For the device unconsciously formed according to an organic image serves in turn as the image for clarifying and understanding the organism from which it takes its origins.[8]

In less Teutonic prose, technology becomes more significant and comprehensible once man realizes that in it he has projected his own body.

Kapp analyzes a number of specific devices as examples of what he calls "organ projection," such as the axe, an extension of the arm. He posits an affinity between the electrical systems in nerves and electrical devices and discusses the projection of man's nervous system at some length. With regard to the telegraph cable, he writes:

> Its comparison with the function of the nervous system goes without saying. It is in general use, in order to make apparent the behavior of the electric current in the organism. Our conceptions of nerves and of electrical cables are so covered in ordinary life that one may justly assert that there exists no other mechanical device which reproduces more precisely its organic prototype, and, on the other hand, there is no organ whose inner constitution is so obviously formed according to it, as the

8. Ibid., pp. 25–28.

. . . strands in the telegraph cable. Organ projection celebrates a great triumph here.[9]

And to make the triumph more striking, Kapp juxtaposes sketches of a cross section of a cable and of a nerve.

But he did live in the nineteenth century, and in his sporadic literalism, he shows himself a man of his age. Thus, he compares railroads to blood vessels, and interprets literacy and the telegraph as extensions of the finger. No matter what kind of writing we consider:

The principal thing always remains the extant image of the active finger's natural ability to write as [i.e., in the form of a] stylus, crayon, reed, chisel, and quill.[10]

For Kapp, the telegraph consists of a sender and a receiver; he has forgotten his own reference to the extensions of the nervous system in the cables that connect the two. Despite his extensive discussions of the unconscious, and his references to the psychic implications of technology, he never mentions the possible unconscious effects of the application of technology to language itself.

Thus Kapp's pioneering work has great historical interest and deserves more recognition than it now receives. Friedrich Dessauer sums up Kapp's significance very well:

Kapp sensed and touched on something important but could not clearly see what now comes distinctly and articulately to light: in the infinitely complicated organic models and processes whose essence is not comprehensible, there are analogies *of a relational nature,* relational analogies to technological processes.[11]

While Kapp sensed the importance of dealing with relationships, he could not himself do so, and his work remains a collection of parts that never becomes a whole. He can never keep the promises of the subtitle of *Outlines,* which is *Toward the History of the Rise of Culture from New Viewpoints,* partially because of his verbosity and literal analogies, but primarily because he fails to integrate his own emphasis on the unconscious effects of technology with his concept of technology as organ projection.

9. Ibid., pp. 139–40.
10. Ibid., p. 292.
11. Friedrich Dessauer, *Streit um die Technik,* p. 421. Dessauer's emphasis.

My treatment of Bergson as the crucial twentieth-century theoretician of technology will come as a surprise only to those who accept the cliché that he propounded irrationalism and mysticism. Bergson's longtime concern with technology derives from his desire to create concepts that would allow people to think in holistic terms; and his own insistence on flux as the essence of experience ultimately forced him to think about technological change. Since he related all change to biological change, or evolution, he had to make sense of technology in terms of evolution, and thus he had to deal with the challenge of Darwin's linear concepts of evolution.

Kuhn states very well the dilemma that Darwin's work posed for Bergson. After commenting that in pre-Darwinian evolutionary theories "Each new stage of evolutionary development was a more perfect realization of a plan that had been present from the start," he continues:

> For many men the abolition of that teleological kind of
> evolution was the most significant and least palatable of
> Darwin's suggestions. *The Origin of Species* recognized no goal
> set either by God or nature. Instead, natural selection, operating
> in the given environment and with the actual organisms
> presently at hand, was responsible for the gradual but steady
> emergence of more elaborate, further articulated, and vastly
> more specialized organisms. (pp. 171–72)

That is to say, Darwinian evolution consisted of pure sequence. As we know, Bergson found pure sequence unacceptable. I now wish to show how he made technology essential in coherent, nonlinear concepts of change.

Significantly, Bergson's first discussion of technology occurs in a section of *Creative Evolution,* which is entitled "The Directions of Evolution." In order to understand the nature of his subsequent treatment of evolution, one needs to keep in mind his statement, *"Instinct and intellect thus represent two divergent* [but] *equally elegant solutions to one and the same problem"* (p. 616). Faced with the challenge of the extreme linearity of Darwinian evolution, Bergson treats instinct and intellect not as a dichotomy, as he usually does, but as a binary pair.

The section of his work that concerns us here begins with the question, "At what date can we show the appearance of man on earth?" (p. 611). Since the appearance of man, like everything else, occurred as process, Bergson changes the definition of man from *Homo sapiens* to *Homo faber* (p. 613). Thus, he can answer his own question by saying, "At the time when the first weapons and the first tools were made" (p. 611). The making of weapons and tools must have taken the form of a conscious act, and Bergson associates it with the appearance of consciousness, and of intellect. Man did not of course cease to evolve after he made the first tool, but he evolved in a way that combined instinct and intellect. Thus:

> Instinct is . . . necessarily specialized, being only the utilization of a determined object for a determined goal. On the other hand, the instrument made by intelligence is an imperfect instrument. It is obtained only at the cost of effort. It is almost always difficult to manage. However, as it is made of unorganized matter, it can take any form, serve any purpose, free a living being from any difficulty that arises, and confer on it an unlimited number of powers. Inferior to the natural instrument for the satisfaction of immediate needs, it has the advantage over it that the need is less pressing. Above all, it reacts on the nature of the being which makes it, since in calling on it to exercise a new function, it confers on it, so to speak, a richer organization, being an artificial organ which extends [*prolonge*] the natural organism. For every need which it satisfies, it creates a new need, and thus instead of closing the circle of action where an animal moves automatically, like instinct, it opens an indefinite field to this activity where it pushes it [the activity] further and further, and makes it more and more free. (pp. 614–15)

Bergson is reasoning logically here from the premise that perception operates as a circuit. Thus any tool or any made thing "confers . . . a richer organization." In stating that the tool "opens an indefinite field," Bergson is thinking of a distinction between making and organizing, which occurs in his section "L'élan vital": "Making . . . goes from the periphery to the center, or, as the philosophers would say, from the many to the one. On the other hand, the work of organization goes from the center to the periphery" (pp. 573–74). Instinct organizes, from the one to the many; intellect makes, from the many to the one.

Since the binary pair past–present operates here, too, "A century has passed since the invention of the steam engine, and we are only beginning to feel the deep dislocation which it has given us. The revolution which has occurred in industry has disrupted the relations between people to no less a degree" (p. 612). Bergson has so many other concerns in *Creative Evolution* that he did not develop this suggestive remark and took it up again only in his last book, *The Two Sources of Religion and Morality* (1932).

By the thirties, many more of the effects of industrialization had become apparent; this held true particularly for the disruption of the relations between people brought about by totalitarianism. Bergson discusses thoughtfully the advantages of technology in satisfying humanity's needs but senses that arguments about technology usually miss the point: "We are taken with an accidental effect, [and] do not see the machine world [*la machinisme*] in what it should be, in its essence" (p. 1238). Bergson, however, thinks in paradigms, and he begins by repeating his concept of technology:

> If our organs are natural instruments, our instruments are by the same token, artificial organs. The workman's tool continues his hand; mankind's ensemble of tools [*outillage*] is thus a prolongation of his body. Nature, in endowing us with an intellect whose essence is making [not organizing], has thus prepared a certain enlargement for us. (p. 1238)

Now comes the important passage, in which Bergson brings together man's extensions and man's psyche:

> But machines which use gas, charcoal, and oil, and which convert into movement the potential energy accumulated over millions of years, have come to give our organism an extension so vast, and a power so formidable, so disproportionate to its scale and power, that surely it has not been anticipated in the structure of our species: this has created a unique opportunity, man's greatest material success on the planet. A spiritual motive was perhaps imprinted at the beginning; the extensions were made automatically, assisted by an accidental blow of a pickaxe which strikes a miraculous treasure beneath the earth. Thus, in an immeasurably large body, the soul remains as it was, too small now to fill it up, too weak to direct it. Hence the void between the one and the other. Hence the redoubtable social, political, and international problems which are so many definitions of this void, and which evoke so much disorganized effort and inefficiency today: in order to fill it up, there must be new reserves of potential energy, moral energy this time. (pp. 1238–39)

Implicit here, as in Bergson's discussions of comedy as a corrective to social rigidity, is the concept of society—and ultimately, the world —as a single dynamic, interrelated whole. Technology, by increasing humanity's power, has satisfied many of its basic needs (*besoins réels,* as Bergson calls them), and in so doing, has thrown society out of balance. I believe that in this passage Bergson has given the first serious attempt to interpret politics and international relations in a paradigmatic, suprapersonal way by relating them to technological change.

Although no one before McLuhan made these suggestions more concretely, various European thinkers developed certain aspects of them. Ernst Cassirer, whom we take up next, had a mind which constantly searched for synthesis, and thus his *Mythical Thought* (1924) contains themes from Hegel, whom he quotes, and Worringer, Nietzsche, and Bergson, whom he does not quote. Like Worringer, he argues that myths do not copy nature but express man's interaction with it; like Nietzsche, he discusses the individuation of Greek tragedy as the beginning of individual consciousness. But here he begins to resemble Bergson. As Bergson had defined man as *Homo faber,* not *Homo sapiens,* so Cassirer states, "The most important factor in the growth of the consciousness of personality is and remains the factor of *action.*"[12]

When man acts in the context of the natural environment, the binary pair organism–environment becomes extremely important; its operation means that man changes himself by making things.

> As soon as man seeks to influence things not by mere image magic or name magic but through implements, he has undergone an inner crisis—even if, for the present, this influence still operates through the customary channels of magic.[13]

> Thus we see that even if we regard the implement purely in its technical aspect as the fundamental means of building material culture, this achievement, if it is to be truly understood and evaluated in its profoundest meaning, may not be considered in isolation. To its mechanical function there corresponds here again a purely spiritual function which not

12. Ernst Cassirer, *The Philosophy of Symbolic Forms, II. Mythical Thought,* p. 199.
13. Ibid., p. 214.

only develops from the former, but conditions it from the very first and is indissolubly correlated with it. Never does the implement serve simply for the mastery of an outside world which can be regarded as finished, simply given "matter"; rather, it is through the use of the implement that the image, the spiritual, ideal form of this outside world, is created for man.[14]

This reasoning, and its psychological assumptions, have a familiar ring, of course, for Cassirer had read Kapp and generalizes from his work.

The fundamental argument of the philosophy of Symbolic Forms has shown that the concept which Kapp designates as "organ projection" holds a meaning which extends far beyond the technical mastery and knowledge of nature. While the philosophy of technology deals with the immediate and mediated bodily organs by which man gives the outside world its determinate form and imprint, the philosophy of Symbolic Forms is concerned with the totality of spiritual expressive functions. It regards them not as copies of being but as trends and modes of formation, as "organs" less of mastery than of signification. And here again the operation of these organs takes at first a wholly unconscious form. Language, myth, art—each procures from itself its own world of forms which can be understood only as expressions of the spontaneity of the spirit.[15]

To understand technology as a form of spiritual creativity, like language, myth, and art, means to integrate technology into a cognitive paradigm. This, in turn, means understanding the present in terms of this paradigm. No one in the twenties—not even Cassirer—could do this. Only after World War II had forced the implications of technology on everyone's attention did another thinker attempt a similar synthesis.

The title of Jean Gebser's two-volume study, *Origin and Present* (1949–1953), refers to the binary pair past–present; Gebser insists that humanity understand itself "as the totality of its mutations."[16] For Gebser, these mutations include the three major periods of history, "the un-perspectival world," "the perspectival world," and "the aperspectival world." He follows Nietzsche not only in the arrangement of this triad, but also (as the terms indicate) in the use of the eye

14. Ibid., p. 215.
15. Ibid., pp. 216–17.
16. Jean Gebser, *Ursprung und Gegenwart,* 1:246.

as the criterion for distinguishing among them. Thus, the passage from the "un-perspectival world" to the "perspectival world" (the Renaissance, of course) means a change from the ear to the eye.

> That the series: sound, images, signs may be correct is shown by the development of writing, which was first hieroglyphics, a mythic script, and only later a script which used signs or letters. It thus had a mentally abstracting emphasis so that the meaning of a word had to be expressed through pitch and tone before it could be expressed by its sign.[17]

Here we find the beginnings, but only the beginnings, of an integrated theory of literacy as a form of technology.

The second mutation, from "the perspectival world" to the "aperspectival world" means the demise of this visual emphasis.

> He who sees rationally, sees in a fragmenting manner [teilend] —it is important not to forget this fundamental definition of the rational. He who "sees" arationally perceives as far as possible the whole, a "structure of coherence." And this is neither a vital, a psychic, nor a mental-rational manner of procedure, but an integral-spiritual one. Modern art, and with it music and the other disciplines of our age, are striving for this.[18]

As this last sentence suggests, Gebser applies his strong theoretical sense to various disciplines and writes especially well on the resolution of dichotomies into binary pairs. In music, for example, "In the overcoming of the dualism [i.e., dichotomy] of major and minor is reflected, to name only one parallel, the overcoming of the dualism of energy and matter achieved by physics."[19]

Gebser could not have made any of these statements without an awareness of the significance of technology in a holistic system. He assumes that technology has an immediate relationship to the body.

> Insofar as the machine is a renunciation [Entäusserung: literally, an "outering"], that is, the placing out [Hinausstellung] of certain human capacities, it is, in psychological terms, a projection. . . . All making, whether it be sorcery, or the technical, rational construction of a machine, is a renunciation of inner powers or gifts which thereby makes them visible. Every tool, every implement, every machine is only a practical

17. Ibid., p. 476.
18. Ibid., 2:304.
19. Ibid., 2:297.

application (and thus an implication directed by perspective) of laws of the "within" found again in the eye, and precisely the laws of one's own body. . . . Every invention is first of all a placing-out which rediscovers and imitates those regularities which are physiologically appropriate to, and inherent in, the structure of man; by being projected into a tool, these regularities can become conscious.[20]

While Gebser may never have read Kapp, he had read Cassirer and Bergson and like them includes all making, from sorcery to modern technology, as a "placing out" of the body. One can even say that this passage has a familiar quality, for—despite Gebser's encyclopedic knowledge and analytical skill—it has the same abstract quality that we encountered in Kapp and Cassirer. Our final two theorists, Pierre Teilhard de Chardin and Lewis Mumford, have in common their discontent with abstract statements about technology, although their procedures differed greatly.

Teilhard de Chardin made the first serious attempt to relate technological change to man's experience of the transcendent. He thus wished to do for modern man what Cassirer had done for nonliterate peoples in *Mythical Thought*. But Teilhard's training in paleontology gave him the habit of thinking about evolution, and he seems to have understood what he wanted to do in life after reading *Creative Evolution*. He continued Bergson's enterprise of asserting that change occurs, and has occurred, in a meaningful way. Since he believed in science and religion with equal fervor, he also made explicit the qualities of Bergson's work that have attracted Roman Catholic intellectuals for many years. While I cannot rival the completeness of Madeleine Barthélemy-Modaule's book on Teilhard's relationship to Bergson,[21] I wish to give some account of Teilhard's vision of evolution in order to make his thought on technology meaningful.

In imagistic terms, to resolve dichotomies into binary pairs means to bend lines into circles. Teilhard does this in *The Phenomenon of Man* by integrating Bergson's distinction between making, which goes from the many to the one, and organizing, which goes from the one to the many, into the process of evolution. Any given period in what Teilhard calls "the tree of life" begins with a group of very similar creatures, which form a "peduncle," or stalk. The creatures very, very

20. Ibid., 1:210–11.
21. Madeleine Barthélemy-Modaule, *Bergson et Teilhard de Chardin.*

gradually differentiate into heterogeneous groups, or "verticils"—
groups arranged around a point on an axis. All but one of the groups
that form the verticil die off, and the remaining phylum then branches
out to form a new peduncle in the succeeding period, during which
the same pattern works itself out again. In the following passage,
Teilhard assumes that "tangential energy" (making) creates verticils,
and that "radial energy" (organizing) creates peduncles.

> To avoid a fundamental dualism, at once impossible and
> anti-scientific, and at the same time to safeguard the natural
> complexity of the stuff of the universe, I accordingly propose
> the following as a basis for all that is to emerge later.
> We shall assume that, essentially, all energy is psychic in
> nature; but add that in each particular element this fundamental
> energy is divided into two distinct components: a *tangential
> energy* which links the element with all others of the same
> order (that is to say, of the same complexity and the same
> centricity) as itself in the universe; and a *radial energy* which
> draws it toward ever greater complexity and centricity—in other
> words forwards.[22]

Like Eliot and the other modernists, Teilhard sought coherence in
history in the form of binarism. Whereas Eliot, as a poet, thought about
cultural history, Teilhard, as a scientist, thought about cosmic history.

In interpreting man's place in the cosmos, Teilhard continues
Bergson's interest in the rise of consciousness, and does so in a
very Bergsonian manner: "Discontinuity in continuity: that is how,
in the theory of its mechanism, the birth of thought, like that of
life, presents itself and refines itself."[23] In this discontinuity, the
being that became man acquired consciousness, and consciousness
forms a circle.

> By this individuation of himself in the depths of himself, the
> living element, which heretofore had been spread out and
> divided over a diffuse circle of perceptions and activities, was
> constituted for the first time as a *centre* in the form of a point
> at which all the impressions knit themselves together and fuse
> into a unity that is conscious of its own organization.[24]

22. Pierre Teilhard de Chardin, *The Phenomenon of Man,* pp. 64–65.
Here and elsewhere, I retain Teilhard's emphasis and capitalization, as well as
his British translator's spelling.
23. Ibid., p. 169.
24. Ibid., p. 165.

In Bergson, the organizing qualities of instinct are not conscious. Teilhard's difference with Bergson here anticipates a further difference in the use of technology.

In a binary system, individual events do not occur; one "reflection upon itself" implies a second reflection. Thus, the second reflection—of all the centers this time—will take place at what Teilhard calls Omega: "By its structure Omega, in its ultimate principle, can only be a *distinct Centre radiating at the core of a* system of centres."[25] Since "technics has a biological role,"[26] technology, as a making that moves from the many to the one, actually anticipates Omega, by extending and unifying mankind. "Thanks to the prodigious biological event represented by the discovery of electromagnetic waves, each individual finds himself henceforth (actively and passively) simultaneously present over land and sea, in every corner of the earth."[27] And since Teilhard very rarely thinks in dichotomies, he understands that the extensions of mankind evolve with mankind.

> Take the case of the locomotive, the dynamo, aviation, cinema, radio—whatever. Is it not evident that these numerous devices are born and develop, successively and together, from roots in a prior world-wide mechanical state? For a long time, there have no longer been either isolated inventors nor isolated machines. But, more and more, every machine comes into being as a function of all other machines of the earth, and, more and more again, all the machines of the earth taken together tend to form a single structured, large Machine. Necessarily obeying the inflexion of zoological phyla, the mechanical phyla turn inward in their turn in the case of Man, thus accelerating and multiplying their progress until they form a single giant complex girdling the earth. And the basis, the inventive core of this new apparatus, what is it, if not precisely the thinking nucleus of the Noosphere?
>
> When *Homo faber* appeared, in an elementary form, the tool was born as an externalized appendage of the human body. Today the tool has been transformed into a mechanized envelope (coherent within itself and immensely varied) of all Humanity.[28]

25. Ibid., p. 262.
26. Pierre Teilhard de Chardin, "Place de la Technologie dans une Biologie Générale de L'Humanité," in *L'Activation de l'Énergie,* p. 166.
27. Teilhard de Chardin, *The Phenomenon of Man,* p. 240.
28. Teilhard de Chardin, *L'Avenir de l'Homme,* pp. 212–13.

By developing Bergson's work, Teilhard has created a profoundly moving and intellectually elegant vision of humanity's evolution through its extensions of itself; but like Bergson himself, and in a manner consistent with a long-standing tradition of French prose, Teilhard does not deal with the meaning of technology as the immediate data of consciousness. As Walter Ong once remarked to me, European intellectuals usually have very little direct experience of technology, whereas Americans grow up with it. Therefore it would be well to make some summary observations on an American writer and thinker who has a marvelous sensitivity to the quality of everyday life—Lewis Mumford.

As with Teilhard, so with Mumford: only a small part of the lifework of a wonderful, inspired, and inspiring man has immediate relevance here. I wish merely to show that Mumford treats technology as the extension of man, that his evaluations of cultural history imply the now familiar modernist admiration for the Middle Ages, rejection of the Renaissance, and dissociation of the Renaissance from the twentieth century and that he continues some of the concerns of Bergson and Nietzsche.

Mumford himself provides an excellent general assessment of his holistic methodology, in an introduction (written in 1963) to the paperback edition of his first major work, *Technics and Civilization* (1932):

> *Technics and Civilization* broke with this traditional neglect of technology [in history]: it not merely summarized for the first time the technical history of the last thousand years of Western civilization, but revealed the constant interplay between the social milieu—monasticism, capitalism, science, play, luxury, war—and the more specific achievements of the inventor, the industrialist, and the engineer.[29]

Mumford is not making an idle boast here. He calls on his seemingly inexhaustible knowledge of Western society to examine the changes that technology has created in human experience.

In his treatment of the nature of technology, and of its effects, Mumford closely follows Bergson, as in these lines from *Technics and Civilization*:

29. Lewis Mumford, "Introduction," *Technics and Civilization,* n.p.

In back of the development of tools and machines lies the attempt to modify the environment in such a way as to fortify and sustain the human organism: the effort is either to extend the powers of the otherwise unarmed organism, or to manufacture outside of the body a set of conditions more favorable toward maintaining its equilibrium and ensuring its survival. Instead of a physiological adaptation to the cold, like the growth of hair or the habit of hibernation, there is an environmental adaptation, such as that which is made possible by the use of clothes and the erection of shelters.[30]

Note with interest Mumford's use of the word *equilibrium* in this statement, for it denotes another assumption that Mumford shares with Bergson, but that he integrates into his work more completely than did Bergson: the concept of a society as a dynamic, interrelated whole that seeks to maintain a balance among its parts. (Mumford certainly encountered this idea in the work of other writers in addition to Bergson, but this fact does not concern us here.)

Mumford finds this equilibrium characteristic of the medieval city, and from *Sticks and Stones* (1924) through *The City in History* (1962), he never tires of presenting the advantages of the medieval village over the modern city. Furthermore, he makes this typically modernist judgment with a distinctly American accent; for Mumford, "The capital example of the medieval tradition lies in the New England village."[31] That sentence occurs in *Sticks and Stones;* these comments from *The City in History* develop the same idea:

The New England town deliberately refused to grow beyond the possibility of socializing and assimilating its members: it thus brought into existence, and in many places kept going for two centuries, a balance between rural and urban occupations, as well as an internal balance of population and usable land.[32]

But this balance did not, of course, last indefinitely. Like a good modernist, Mumford asserts: "In order to understand the post-medieval town, one must be on guard against the still fashionable interpreta-

30. Ibid., p. 10.
31. Lewis Mumford, *Sticks and Stones: A Study of American Architecture and Civilization,* p. 13.
32. Lewis Mumford, *The City in History,* p. 332.

tion of the Renascence as a movement toward freedom and the reestablishment of the dignity of man."[33]

In describing the change of thought patterns that occurred during the Renaissance, Mumford must surely have had Eliot, and the title of his most famous poem, in mind when he wrote, in *Technics and Civilization:*

> By confining his operations to those aspects of reality which had, so to say, market value, and by isolating and dismembering the corpus of experience, the physical scientist created a habit of mind favorable to discrete practical inventions: at the same time it was highly unfavorable to all those forms of art for which the secondary qualities and the individualized receptors and motivators of the artists were of fundamental importance. . . .
>
> What was left was the bare, depopulated world of matter and motion: a wasteland. . . . By renouncing a large part of his humanity, a man could achieve godhood: he dawned on this second chaos and created the machine in his own image: the image of power, but power ripped loose from his flesh and isolated from his humanity.[34]

In his discussions of media in the paleotechnic complex, his term for post-Renaissance society, Mumford summarizes all this as a principle that corresponds to what Bergson said in *The Two Sources* (which was published in the same year as *Technics and Civilization*): *"In projecting one side of the human personality into the concrete forms of the machine, we have created an independent environment that has reacted upon every other side on the personality."*[35]

Rather like Nietzsche in *The Genealogy of Morals,* Mumford devotes a good deal of energy to investigating the effects of the individuation of binary pairs into dichotomies. I find his discussions of the dichotomies in the baroque city, in *The City in History,* for example, most perceptive. Moreover, he continues Nietzsche's association of individuation and the eye: "The medieval symbolism dissolved and the world became a different place as soon as one looked at it through glasses."[36] Or, to make the same point in a different way: "Glasses

33. Ibid., p. 345.
34. Mumford, *Technics and Civilization,* p. 51.
35. Ibid., p. 324. Mumford's emphasis.
36. Ibid., p. 126.

not merely opened people's eye but minds: seeing was believing.
. . . Now the eye became the most respected organ."[37] In his superb
section on glass, Mumford analyzes the new attitudes created by
visual orientation:

> Self-consciousness, introspection, mirror-conversation developed
> with the new object itself: this preoccupation with one's image
> comes at the threshhold of the mature personality when young
> Narcissus gazes long and deep into the face of the pool—and
> the sense of the separate personality, a perception of the
> objective attributes of one's identity, grows out of this
> communion.[38]

This perception of the objective attributes of one's identity occurred
at the same time as a crucial invention.

> Printing was from the beginning a completely mechanical
> achievement. Not merely that: it was the type for all future
> instruments of reproduction: for the printed sheet, even before
> the military uniform, was the first completely standardized
> product, manufactured in series, and the movable types
> themselves were the first example of completely standardized
> and interchangeable parts. Truly a revolutionary invention in
> every department.[39]

Mumford wanted so much to do justice to long-neglected aspects of
technology that he could not deal with literacy as a phenomenon,
although he obviously anticipates McLuhan's treatment of it. McLuhan was thirteen years old when Mumford published *Sticks and
Stones,* in which he deals with the effect of literacy on architecture
in the following way:

> Victor Hugo said in Notre Dame that the printing-press
> destroyed architecture, which had hitherto been the stone
> record of mankind. The real misdemeanor of the printing-press,
> however, was not that it took literary values away from
> architecture, but that it caused architecture to derive its value
> from literature. With the Renaissance the great modern
> distinction between the literate and the illiterate extends even to
> building; the master mason who knew his stone and his

37. Ibid., p. 127.
38. Ibid., p. 129.
39. Ibid., p. 135.

workmen and his tools gave way to the architect who knew his Palladio and his Vignola and his Vitruvius.[40]

Such explications as this rarely occur, however, because Mumford rarely discusses art, artists, and works of art.

Individuation, like the equilibrium of the medieval town and the New England village, did not last indefinitely. Mumford, like most modernists, believes that we live in an age of reintegration (Nietzsche's reappearance of tragedy). Mumford's sense of the nascent equilibrium of large cities, like Teilhard's intimation of Omega, comes from electricity:

> Technologically, two of the most perfect examples of this new network are in our power and communications systems: particularly clear in the electric power grid. . . .
>
> Each unit in this system has a certain degree of self-sufficiency and self-direction, equal to ordinary occasions. But by being linked together, the power stations form a whole system whose parts, though relatively independent, can upon demand work as a whole, and make good what is lacking in any particular area. The demand may be made at any point in the system, and the whole may be drawn on to respond to it.[41]

These new interrelationships resolve into a single binary pair, village–world, the dichotomies by which people formerly gave themselves social definitions.

> We must now conceive the city, accordingly, not primarily as a place of business or government, but as an essential organ for expressing and actualizing the new human personality—that of "One World Man." The old separation of man and nature, of townsman and foreigner, of Greek and barbarian, of citizen and foreigner, can no longer be maintained: for communication, the entire planet is becoming a village; and as a result, the smallest neighborhood or precinct must be planned as a working model of the larger world.[42]

Mumford published *The City in History* in 1962, the same year in which McLuhan published *The Gutenberg Galaxy,* where he first uses the term *global village.* As has happened so often, the thoughts of gifted men of our century coincided. This coincidence amounts to an

40. Mumford, *Sticks and Stones,* p. 41.
41. Mumford, *The City in History,* p. 565.
42. Ibid., p. 573.

affinity of sensibility between McLuhan and Mumford, who both have striking (if radically different) writing styles, wide-ranging knowledge, and great sensitivity toward the manifestations of cultural change.

Holistic concepts logically lead one to think of the world as a unit, and of electrical technology as its binding force. Gebser, the most scholarly of the theorists in this chapter, thinks of the world in this way no less than Teilhard. General agreement also exists that the effect of technology goes inward as well as outward. People *think* differently after they have extended themselves through technology.

So far I have dealt with the growth of the nonlinear paradigm from the initial statements of principle in Bergson and Nietzsche up to *Understanding Media*. The various elements of the paradigm that McLuhan used—the interpretation of art as cognition, of technology as the extension of man, and the tripartite scheme of historical under-standing—had, by 1964, the year when *Understanding Media* ap-peared, received crucial acceptance among the theorists whose work had already touched on the elements. McLuhan added very little in a conceptual sense. He did not need to, for the elements of the paradigm had received validation through consensus. McLuhan did two things: he synthesized the previously disparate elements, and he applied them, with great wit and imagination, to the immediate data of consciousness. How he did this is the subject of the next section.

Part III.

Understanding Media

Chapter **8**

The Maturation of the Nonlinear Paradigm in *Understanding Media*

This chapter will analyze both McLuhan's continuity with the various aspects of the nonlinear paradigm, as the preceding chapters have developed it, and his new syntheses, which give a more complete statement of the paradigm. My purpose here is to present McLuhan's system as an integrated whole, not to explicate or apply it. In doing so, I will emphasize the similarities between McLuhan and the work of Bergson and Nietzsche, rather than the better-known ones between McLuhan and Wyndham Lewis, or between McLuhan and the Canadian economic historian Harold Innis. Although many statements in the work of these others anticipate similar statements in *Understanding Media,* McLuhan's writing consistently differs from theirs in its greater specificity.

McLuhan's similarities to Bergson frequently appear when he discusses the interrelated topics of technology, time, and the nature of the artist's work. With regard to technology, the very subtitle of *Understanding Media, The Extensions of Man,* recalls Bergson's formulations of technology as extensions of man in *The Two Sources of Religion and Morality.* Since Kapp's work remained unknown except to a few German specialists, it is reasonable to assume that McLuhan originally found the concept in Bergson; he certainly studied its use in Mumford and Teilhard de Chardin. Moreover, McLuhan's interest in, and analyses of, myth as a form of response to technological change relates his work to that of Cassirer.

Because a consensus already existed on this matter, McLuhan himself did not have to think through this concept, and hence he hardly discusses it as such. He gives a complete statement of the principle for the first time halfway through the book: "The transformations of technology have the character of organic evolution because all technologies are extensions of our physical being." (p. 182).[1] Thus

1. Page numbers after quotations from McLuhan refer to: Marshall McLuhan, *Understanding Media.*

stated, the principle remains an abstraction; to make use of it, one must assume, as McLuhan (following Bergson) does, that society coheres as a dynamic, interrelated whole. McLuhan implies as much when he writes: "The use of any kind of medium or extension of man alters the patterns of interdependence among people, as it alters the ratios among our senses" (p. 90). McLuhan is making explicit the implicit analogy in Bergson between the psyche and the society as integrated wholes. The phrase "the ratio among the senses" relates technology to the structure of the psyche:

> An extension appears to be an amplification of an organ, a
> sense or a function, that inspires the central nervous system to a
> self-protective numbing of the extended area, at least so far as
> direct inspection and awareness are concerned. (p. 172)

Bergson's work has exerted such enormous influence in the twentieth century because he stated very suggestive principles, and he left them at that. Whereas Bergson tentatively suggested in *The Two Sources* that international tensions result from technological change, McLuhan (here following a hint from Harold Innis) gives specific historical applications: "That Hitler came into political existence at all is directly owing to radio and public-address systems" (p. 300).

The phrase "organic evolution" in McLuhan's definition of technology as the extensions of man refers to another assumption that McLuhan shares with Bergson (and with relativity theory), that everything exists as process. Typically, however, he expresses this sense of process with a joke, as the more sober Bergson would never have done: "A caterpillar gazing at the butterfly is supposed to have remarked, 'Waal, you'll never catch me in one of those durn things'" (p. 34). From the nature of process follows an awareness of the arbitrariness of clock time, a major Bergsonian theme. A belief in the uniformity of time leads one to think that a given experience or situation will go on repeating itself indefinitely, a proposition that McLuhan denies in the final sentence of *Understanding Media:* "Panic about automation as a threat of uniformity on a world scale is the projection into the future of mechanical standardization and specialism, which are now past" (p. 359). McLuhan's work often takes the form of an analysis of this phenomenon, which he calls "rearview mirrorism"— looking ahead, but seeing the past. This insistence that people perceive the past in the present recalls Bergson's musings on the role of the unconscious in *The Two Sources:* "The present, perceived in the past like a mirage, is thus that which we call the unconscious in general. The retro-active quality of the present is at the origin of many philosophical illusions" (p. 1237). Or, as McLuhan put it in his simpler and more general way, "Non-artists always look at the present through the spectacles of the preceding age" (p. 243).

McLuhan's term "non-artists" suggests a relationship between what Eliot would have called "artistic sensibility" and Bergsonian *durée,* or the binary interaction of the past and the present. Bergson states in the *Essay,* "We are free when our acts emanate from our entire personality, when they express it, when they have to them that indefinable resemblance which one occasionally finds between the artist and his work" (p. 113). McLuhan has both a more general and a more specific version of this principle: "The artist is the man in any field, scientific or humanistic, who grasps the implications of his actions and of new knowledge in his own time. He is the man of integral awareness" (p. 65). If the artist has an integral awareness because he understands the difference between the present and the past, how does this integral awareness function in society?

McLuhan's general concept of the artist derives partially from Bergson, and partially from Wyndham Lewis, as we will learn presently. Essentially, McLuhan combines two of Bergson's statements about art in *Laughter:* that the artist tears the veil from reality, and that laughter counteracts rigidity. Now "tearing the veil from reality" has a static, visual quality that we rarely find in Bergson. While McLuhan retains this emphasis on the cognitive function of art, he also construes this cognition as cognition of a process of technological change. In such a process, rigidity occurs when people fail to understand that a new system of interrelationships has replaced the old one. All innovative art, not just comedy, counteracts this societal rigidity.

> At any rate, in experimental art, men are given the exact specifications of coming violence to their own psyches from their own counter-irritants of technology. For those parts of ourselves that we thrust out in the form of new invention are attempts to counter or neutralize collective pressures and irritations. But the counter-irritant usually proves a greater plague than the initial irritant, like a drug habit. And it is here that the artist can show us how to "ride with the punch,"

> instead of "taking it on the chin." It can only be repeated that
> human history is a record of "taking it on the chin." (p. 66)

Here, the integral awareness that characterizes the artist enables him
to respond to any process on its own terms. Notice that rigidity gives
rise to violence; if art can help avoid this violence, it serves a vital need
in society. McLuhan, like Eliot, Pound, and many other modernists,
insists on the utility of art above all.

McLuhan's affinities with Bergson make sense in a religious as
well as in an intellectual context. Although Bergson did not convert
to Roman Catholicism, he deeply sympathized with its tenets and
provided a major stimulus for the Catholic Revival in early twentieth-
century France, and especially for Teilhard de Chardin. McLuhan's
Catholicism, and his friendship of many years' standing with Walter
Ong, associates him with this movement. Ong (both in conversations
with me and on several public occasions) has emphasized the importance of McLuhan's formative years when he taught at St. Louis University. Clearly, then, *Understanding Media* comes out of a profoundly Catholic context, and it might seem that McLuhan should
have little in common with Nietzsche. But to say this is to oversimplify
twentieth-century intellectual history.

McLuhan refers only indirectly to his Catholicism, in one of the
few personal statements in *Understanding Media:* "There is a deep
faith to be found in this new attitude—a faith that concerns the ultimate harmony of all being. Such is the faith in which this book has
been written" (pp. 5–6). He might almost be paraphrasing Nietzsche's
statement: "I have christened with the name Dionysus the faith that
in the totality everything redeems and affirms itself" (77:173). Nietzsche's vehemence came not from a lack of faith but from his visceral
sense of outrage at the denial of that faith, primarily in Kantian philosophy. Catholicism is only one possible form of faith in "the ultimate
harmony of all being," as McLuhan puts it. The modernists' admiration for the Middle Ages, as well as their interest in oriental art and
various occult teachings, derives from a similar faith. Without some
form of faith in coherence (often unsystematized and usually nonreligious), modernists would not have taken such an interest in Hegel and
Marx, nor could structuralism have come into being. One does not
study systems without believing in the internal coherence of those
systems.

"From the time of the telegraph onward . . . Western man began to live an implosion. He began suddenly with Nietzschean insouciance to play the movie of his 2,500-year explosion backward" (p. 270). In these two sentences, McLuhan associates the new oral quality of the electric age with Nietzsche's concept of the Dionysian. Numerous relationships occur between the two. If we recall Nietzsche's emphasis on the chorus in Greek tragedy as an essential expression of the Dionysian, we realize that both McLuhan and Nietzsche assume an integrated, pluralistic society and that the essential experiences of that society are communal and shared.

Nietzsche used Wagner as a sign of the return of the Dionysian, as McLuhan uses modern art-as-cognition as a sign of the new oral world. Moreover, McLuhan follows modernism in adapting the tripartite cultural paradigm of *The Birth of Tragedy*. Like the modernists, McLuhan divides Western cultural history into the pre-Renaissance, post-Renaissance, and modern (since about 1900) periods. The modernists attacked the Renaissance and its various artistic expressions, as Nietzsche attacked Kantian idealism. This attitude now seems an unnecessary dichotomy, but it had an important historical function: it sufficiently distanced post-modernists like McLuhan from the Renaissance, so that he could analyze it as a cultural phenomenon. The Renaissance seemed all the more reprehensible to the modernists because they perceived it as a capricious, random phenomenon. Without a theory of technology, they could not understand it in holistic terms. If, however, one integrates Nietzsche's historical paradigm with Bergson's theory of technology, as McLuhan does, it makes sense:

> Print technology transformed the medieval zero into the Renaissance infinity, not only by convergence—perspective and vanishing point—but by bringing into play for the first time in human history the factor of exact repeatability. (p. 116)

Naturally, the twentieth century differs from the post-Renaissance period, not arbitrarily, but because of technology:

> After three thousand years of explosion, by means of fragmenting and mechanical technologies, the Western world is imploding. During the mechanical ages we had extended our bodies in space. Today, after more than a century of electric technology, we have extended our central nervous system itself in a global embrace, abolishing both space and time as far as our planet is concerned. (p. 3)

To be sure, this historical scheme admits of numerous gradations and adaptations, depending on the specific problems one studies. For Nietzsche, the dissolution of the Apollonian and the Dionysian into a dichotomy—McLuhan's explosion—began with Socrates. To take another example, one can define the Middle Ages as a chirographic culture—one that has script but not movable type. Literacy in these conditions cannot spread rapidly, and operates at what Ong calls "low intensity."

Nietzsche associates the Dionysian with myth, as McLuhan associates the new age of electricity with myth: "Myth is contraction of implosion of any process, and the instant speed of electricity confers the mythic dimension on ordinary industrial and social action today" (p. 25). Moreover, McLuhan reads myth as a structure that "Capsulates a prolonged process into a flashing insight" (p. 82), a formulation that closely resembles Nietzsche's concept of myth in *The Birth of Tragedy* as "the concentrated world image [*das zusammengezogene Weltbild*]" (70:179).

Finally, McLuhan's style owes a good deal to Nietzsche. His writing certainly does not resemble Innis's dense prose, and generally lacks the spleen of his favorite of Wyndham Lewis's books, *Time and Western Man*. McLuhan's use of paradox and nonsequitur and his uncanny ability to compress meaning into striking phrases recall Nietzsche's similar gifts and distinguish him from Bergson. McLuhan could well adopt Nietzsche's saying "All good things laugh" (75:326), for he embodies important sociocultural analysis in lines like "The prostitute was a specialist, and the call-girl is not" (p. 266), or "Europe never had adolescents. It had chaperones" (p. 302). Of course, the futurists and the Dadaists made good use of striking phrases, but they too learned from Nietzsche, and in any case took themselves too seriously to play the role of the jester-teacher.

These comments have related McLuhan to his modernist heritage, but have done so only by ignoring his great achievement of synthesis, and to this we now turn. In his chapter on automation, McLuhan gives a key to a historical understanding of his own accomplishments when he says: "It [electric technology] ends the old dichotomies between culture and technology, between art and commerce, and between work and leisure" (pp. 346–47). Like electricity, McLuhan resolves dichotomies, both those of the continuous and those of the noncontinuous subsets of the linear paradigm.

Essentially, the continuous subset of the linear paradigm states that the world consists of identities: things are the same as other things, just as each section of space, or each moment of time, is the same as any other. The continuous subset of the linear paradigm typically views any phenomenon as an undifferentiated mass of similar entities. By making structural distinctions, McLuhan creates binary pairs in three major concepts—perception, technology, and history—which have often remained undifferentiated.

Before analyzing McLuhan's binary pairs, it might be helpful to note that he always assumes that "At no period in human history have men understood the psychic mechanisms involved in invention and technology" (p. 352). The interpreter who understands this interaction of the conscious and the unconscious will pay little attention to what people *thought* about their responses to technology and will not use these people's terms and concepts except as material for analysis. As it often happens, McLuhan is applying a familiar principle to unfamiliar material. Psychologists and linguists take it for granted that people cannot articulate their own psychological and linguistic patterns (that is, these scholars use the binary pair material–analysis), but hardly anyone since Kapp has insisted on the vital role of the unconscious in technology and related matters.

In the linear paradigm, "perception," for all practical purposes, means vision. As we know, however, people in the late nineteenth century began to distinguish between sound and sight, as in Nietzsche's use of the Cyclops' eye as an image of fragmentation. McLuhan says: "The ear is hyperesthetic compared to the neutral eye. The ear is intolerant, closed, and exclusive [integrative], whereas the eye is open, neutral, and associative [fragmenting]" (p. 303). Given the distinction between the ear and the eye, it applies very meaningfully to the distinction between the spoken and the printed word. *Understanding Media* assumes that the spoken and the printed word are not, as the linear paradigm would have it, the same thing. This distinction only begins the analysis, however, for McLuhan continues by associating the ear with touch, and, hence, involvement. The argument goes as follows: The spoken word truly exists only in the binary form of dialogue. Dialogue, in turn, has the same binary form as electricity, by means of which the nervous system as a whole functions. Sound is related to touch. Hence, "Electricity offers a means of getting in touch with every facet of being at once, like the brain itself. Electricity is only incidentally visual and auditory; it is primarily tactile" (p. 249).

The opposition of tactile and visual informs, of course, the more famous opposition between cool and hot media. Since technology functions as the extension of man, it extends him in two essentially different ways—through sight or through touch.

> There is a basic principle that distinguishes a hot medium like radio from a cool one like the telephone, or a hot medium like the movie from a cool one like TV. A hot medium is one that extends one single sense in "high definition." High definition is the state of being well filled with data. A photograph is, visually, "high definition." A cartoon is "low definition," simply because very little information is provided. (p. 22)

The eye perceives passively; the hand, actively. McLuhan therefore defines flat, highly delineated planes as "hot"; they have so much information, i.e., nuances of detail, that we need bring little to them; they are suited to the eye. On the other hand, we complete surfaces such as wood or stone by touch; by analogy with such surfaces, McLuhan calls images, media, or experiences, which have few nuances of detail, and therefore require our participation, "cool."

McLuhan applies this distinction between hot and cool to history, which he resolves into hot and cool processes and characterizes these processes as "explosion" or "implosion." He introduces the comparison with the processes of atomic physics in a characteristically casual way:

> We know from our own past the kind of energy that is released, as by fission, when literacy explodes the tribal or family unit. What do we know about the social and psychic energies that develop by fusion or implosion when literate individuals are suddenly gripped by an electromagnetic field, such as occurs in the new Common Market pressure in Europe? Make no mistake, the fusion of people who have known individualism and nationalism is not the same process as the fission of "backward" and oral cultures that are just coming to individualism and nationalism. (p. 50)

History, like electricity, consists of energy, and the juxtaposition of different forms—again, like electricity—releases this energy in different processes, as atomic processes do. Bergson made a similar distinction between the process of making, which goes from periphery to center, and organizing, which goes from center to periphery. Implosion and explosion (or fragmentation) also correspond to Teilhard's terms "tangential energy" and "radial energy." As usual, McLuhan's formulations differ from these precisely in their more general meaning and greater applicability.

Historical processes do not have a monistic nature; that is, they do not continue indefinitely without change, just as atomic processes do not. As velocity affects mass, so the speed of a process affects its nature: "The stepping-up of speed from the mechanical to the instant electric form reverses explosion into implosion" (p. 35). Explosion and implosion occur in a complementary fashion, and thus create what Bergson would have called the continuity of time. Neither excludes the other, and both may occur in a given society at a given time. Since the speed-up that changes explosion into implosion strikes McLuhan as the dominant process of his age, he understandably emphasizes it; but implosion can imply explosion as well.

When we turn from the continuous to the noncontinuous subset of the linear paradigm, we find that McLuhan is dealing, not with undifferentiated masses but with explicit dichotomies. For example, he resolves the dichotomy culture–technology into a binary pair in the following manner: "Each new technology creates an environment that is itself regarded as corrupt and degrading. Yet the new one turns its predecessor into an art form" (p. viii). These two simple sentences (which apply Bergson's binary pair past–present) serve as the tuning fork to which all of *Understanding Media* vibrates. If one understands these two sentences, everything else in the book makes sense.

Again like Bergson, McLuhan—here and elsewhere—is not describing an independent reality, but is analyzing perception. Since relativity theory allows no privileged frame of reference, no one paradigm of perception may claim priority or preference. Since everything exists as process and therefore changes, perception changes, too; and changes in art express this change in perception. Hence, McLuhan's statement, "In the history of human culture there is no example of a conscious adjustment of the various factors of personal and social life to new extensions except in the puny and peripheral efforts of artists" (pp. 64–65). He is thinking here of Wyndham Lewis's striking formula, which he cites: "The artist is always engaged in writing a detailed history of the future because he is the only person aware of the nature of the present" (p. 65). This definition of the function of the artist makes sense only if one understands that it implies the binary pairs past–present and present–future. If one knows half of either pair, then one knows its complement as well. Such knowledge requires, of course, an ability to separate the flux of the immediate data of consciousness into these pairs.

Perhaps a specific example of this process from the history of English poetry will suggest the power of this principle. Scholars generally agree that no major English poet wrote nature poetry as such until some time after 1750, whereupon it became a dominant mode for a long period. Such a change signals a change in perception of the environment. Until the middle of the eighteenth century, people generally lived in a largely unchanged natural environment. After that time, however, industrialization and organization began to alter this situation to an unprecedented degree; there resulted a new contrast between a natural world and a man-made world. As a result of this contrast, artists began to perceive the uniqueness of the objects of the natural world—trees, brooks, flowers, and so on. The nature poetry of the romantics occurred as a result. If one understands their work as half of the binary pair natural world–man-made world, one can read romanticism as a form of cognition of the new industrialized society, and of the explosion that produced it.

It now seems to us that the modernists were able to emphasize the binary pair past–present, and to attempt to incorporate the totality of Western culture into their work only by creating the dichotomy high culture–mass culture. And one can define a difference between modernism and post-modernism by saying that post-modernism resolved this dichotomy into a binary pair. The two periods have more structural similarities than dissimilarities, however, because mass culture has the same significance for post-modernism as primitive culture had for modernism. McLuhan and other post-modernists shocked intellectuals by taking mass culture seriously, just as Picasso and other modernists shocked intellectuals by taking primitive culture seriously.

These remarks should make readily comprehensible McLuhan's principle that "Anything that is approached in depth acquires as much depth as the greatest matters" (p. 282). If the medium is the message, and if the paradigm has sufficient power (that is, if it resolves a sufficient number of the relevant dichotomies into binary pairs), one should be able to use it on any material at hand. Thus, McLuhan denies the validity of the dichotomy mass culture–high culture in such sentences as, "The advent of electric media released art from this strait jacket [of the printed word] at once, creating the world of Paul Klee, Picasso, Braque, Einstein, the Marx Brothers, and James Joyce" (p. 54). Naturally, to someone who has gone into this dichotomy, it seems improper to include the Marx Brothers among these mandarins of high culture.

McLuhan's analyses of mass culture as having cognitive value offer instructive examples of the paradigm at work; the following may serve as an example:

> In the special Russian issue of *Life* magazine for September 13, 1963, it is mentioned in Russian restaurants and night clubs, "though the Charleston is tolerated, the Twist is taboo." All this is to say that a country in the process of industrialization is inclined to regard hot jazz as consistent with its developing programs. The cool and involved form of the Twist, on the other hand, would strike such a culture at once as retrograde and incompatible with its new mechanical stress. The Charleston, with its aspect of a mechanical doll agitated by strings, appears in Russia as an avant-garde form. (p. 27)

As usual in *Understanding Media,* the analysis here proceeds by finding the isomorphism between the specific phenomenon and the more general social process, explosion or implosion, as the case may be.

McLuhan once commented that he could best express the structure of *Understanding Media* as an "ideogram."[2] He had in mind, of course, Pound's use of the ideogram as an organizational form for images, poems, and even essays. The concept of a book as an ideogram resolves the dichotomy part–whole into a binary pair, for a holistic structure exists everywhere and nowhere: "One can stop anywhere after the first few sentences, and have the full message, if one is prepared to 'dig' it" (p. 26). Hence, the absence of a statement of "point of view," and of step-by-step exposition; I have taken paradigmatic statements from all parts of McLuhan's book, for they occur throughout. McLuhan was thinking of his own work when he wrote, "Spectator becomes artist in oriental art because he must supply all the connections" (p. vi). One must supply the connections in *Understanding Media,* too. Clearly, McLuhan's ability to write in this way comes from his study of works like Eliot's *The Wasteland* and Joyce's *Ulysses* (in addition to Pound's *Cantos*), which also use a variety of styles and materials, and which also make great demands on the reader.

2. McLuhan made the remark in a letter to Frank Kermode; see Kermode's "Between Two Galaxies," in *McLuhan: Hot and Cool,* p. 177.

Understanding Media also differs from more traditional works of scholarship in that it articulates their paradigms by translating them into terms which their authors do not use, as in this comment: "Throughout *The City in History* Lewis Mumford favors the cool or casually structured towns over the hot and intensely filled-in cities" (p. 29). To articulate a paradigm in this way is to perceive by contrast —an act analogous to turning a medium into an art form. McLuhan does this very often in *Understanding Media*. As the title suggests, he intended the work as a handbook and presumably felt that analyzing examples from his own extensive reading would prove helpful to those who wanted to analyze media and social phenomena for themselves. Some of McLuhan's examples now strike us as dated, naturally, but this matters little, for it is not the "correctness" of a single judgment that is at issue, but the coherence of the system as a whole.

If reality occurs as process, then we can best understand *Understanding Media* as process. It clearly took shape as an outgrowth of British imagism, and—more generally—the epistemological and aesthetic theories of Bergson and Nietzsche. The work has a binary relationship to modernism, then, in that it repeats some essential concerns and concepts of modernism. But now that the age of modernism has passed, it has become possible to articulate its paradigm and thus to use some of the binary pairs that modernism produced to resolve some of its remaining dichotomies into other binary pairs of great suggestiveness. Eliot himself, in "Tradition and the Individual Talent," gave us a valuable suggestion which we can use in doing so.

> The difference between the present and the past is that the conscious present is an awareness of the past in a way and to an extent which the past's awareness of itself cannot show.
>   Someone said, "The dead writers are remote from us because we *know* so much more than they did." Precisely, and they are that which we know.[3]

Analogously, we know more than the modernists (in a general, historical sense) and do not use some of their dichotomies. But they *are* that which we know, and they have made postmodernism and the nonlinear paradigm of our age possible. That we can fully articulate this paradigm distinguishes us from them. Without them, however, we would have had no paradigm to articulate.

3. T. S. Eliot, "Tradition and the Individual Talent," in *Selected Essays,* p. 6. Eliot's emphasis.

Chapter 9

An Explication of the Nonlinear Paradigm

Whereas the previous chapter related *Understanding Media* to the past, this chapter will relate it to the present by showing how the nonlinear paradigm explains some anthropological data on perception in a manner consistent with Chomskian linguistics, and by showing how one can truely understand some of the criticisms of McLuhan.

McLuhan (following Bergson) emphasizes the role of perception, especially sight, in creating his theories of social change. We have various kinds of evidence that people do not all see in the same way and that they do not necessarily see the same things in a given situation. Thus, at the turn of the century, the Viennese art historian Alois Riegl commented in his book *Questions of Style:*

> Travellers often report of Hottentots and Australian Negroes that they cannot recognize their own picture in a drawing or photograph: they can conceive of things only corporeally, but not confined to place.[1]

It might be possible to dismiss such reports, and others like them, as the results of misunderstanding or lack of expertise. However, a recent anthropological study by a group of authors of the problem, *The Influence of Culture on Visual Perception,* tends to verify these casual observations. After administering uniform visual tests to 1,878 informants in all parts of the world, and checking the results by computer, the authors reported:

> For the Muller-Lyer and Sander Parallelogram illusion we put forth the "carpentered-world" hypothesis and an "experience with two-dimensional representation of reality" hypothesis; both of these hypotheses led to the prediction that Western peoples would be more susceptible to these illusions than non-Western

1. Alois Riegl, *Stilfragen,* p. 2.

peoples. We found considerable support for both hypotheses in
our own and others' . . . data.[2]

For the purposes of this discussion, the precise nature of these tests
matters less than the fact that the contrast between "Western" and
"non-Western" peoples amounts to a contrast between literate and
nonliterate peoples. These experimental data tend to give additional
credence to McLuhan's assumption that media affect the organization
of the human sensorium. But the matter cannot rest here, for this
consistency between McLuhan's assumptions and the anthropologists'
data proves relatively little in itself. In order to make the nonlinear
paradigm of *Understanding Media* more cogent, I wish to give a
possible explanation for the genesis and function of these differences
in perception between literate and nonliterate peoples in terms of the
work of a man who was developing his theories at about the same
time as McLuhan—Noam Chomsky.

Since the work of Edward Sapir, Benjamin Whorf, and Ludwig
Wittgenstein (among others), few people have seriously questioned
the proposition that language in some way structures our perception,
although no general agreement exists on how this occurs. I wish
merely to take this assumed relationship as a rationale for applying
Chomsky's theories of the acquisition of language to the acquisition
of culture. However, in so doing, I will make no commitment to
Chomsky's belief that these are linguistic universals or that we learn
our native language readily enough because it corresponds to the
inherent structure of the human mind. No one has as yet proved or
disproved these assumptions, and the argument that I wish to make
proceeds perfectly well without them.

In true postmodernist fashion, Chomsky's theories resolve the
typically modernist dichotomy of synchronic and diachronic analysis
that Ferdinand de Saussure used in his *Course in General Linguistics*,
which created the paradigm for structural linguistics when it appeared
in 1916. By the late fifties, Saussure's emphasis on binary oppositions
in language seemed static to Chomsky, who wanted to create a theory
of linguistic processes and thus needed to explain the nature of dialogue:

The central fact to which any significant linguistic theory must
address itself is this: a mature speaker can produce a new

2. Marshall H. Segall, Donald T. Campbell, and Melville J. Herskovits, *The
Influence of Culture on Visual Perception,* p. 212.

sentence of his language on the appropriate occasion, and other speakers can understand it immediately, though it is equally new to them. Most of our linguistic experience, both as speakers and hearers, is with new sentences; once we have mastered a language, the class of sentences with which we can operate fluently and without difficulty or hesitation is so vast that for all practical purposes (and, obviously, for all theoretical purposes), we may regard it as infinite.[3]

Thus Chomsky is asking, "What makes dialogue possible?" He answers this question by assuming that any new sentence a speaker hears or utters is new only in a trivial sense. It is trivial because he sets up the binary pair of the surface structure of the new sentence and the deep structure of the language:

The grammar as a whole can . . . be regarded as, ultimately, a device for pairing phonetically represented signals with semantic interpretations, this pairing being mediated through a system of abstract structures generated by the syntactic component.[4]

Or, more specifically:

The syntactic component must provide for each sentence (actually, for each interpretation of each sentence) a semantically interpretable *deep structure* and a phonetically interpretable *surface structure* and, in the event that these are distinct, a statement of the relation between these structures.[5]

Although Chomsky developed his now famous theory of generative grammar through the use of symbolic logic and communication theory, his theory lends itself readily to interpretation as an application of Bergson's binary pair past–present. Thus a hearer understands a sentence that he has never heard before because the surface structure of that particular sentence—an experience of the present—conforms to the deep structure of the language that the hearer acquired in the past, as a child. Chomsky argues that children acquire language, not by repeating and repeating the content of specific sentences but by internalizing the subject–verb–object structure that makes this and other such sentences meaningful. In a very Bergsonian manner, then, the past and the present interact to create meaning. Understood in this

3. Noam Chomsky, *Current Issues in Linguistic Theory,* p. 7.
4. Chomsky, *Current Issues,* pp. 9–10.
5. Ibid., p. 10. Chomsky's emphasis.

way, Chomsky's theory of generative grammar presents a specific—but paradigmatic—aspect of the process that anthropologists call "enculturation."

As the authors of *The Influence of Culture on Visual Perception* remind us, "Every human being goes through a process of enculturation, and its effects may be detected as easily in the rebel as in the conformist."[6] During enculturation, society teaches the child not just language, but many other skills as well—how to dress, how to behave in various situations, and so forth. Roland Barthes, in *The Fashion System* and Claude Levi-Strauss, in *The Raw and the Cooked,* have used a methodology derived from that of structural linguistics to make meaningful these nonverbal patterns of social behavior. If we can understand behavior in a manner similar to that by which we understand linguistics, may we not also understand the genesis of language similarly to that of behavior?

We may begin by assuming the existence of a very large, but presumably finite, number of interrelated deep structures that generate behavior the society considers appropriate.[7] These deep structures will vary in many respects, of course. Some, like those of language, remain permanently in effect, while others, such as those that generate social behavior, may operate only during certain stages of growth. But this general statement of the theory need not take such discriminations into account. It must suffice to say that as children internalize the deep structure of their language, they are also internalizing these other deep structures of behavior.

Now if we assume, as McLuhan does, an essential difference between hearing a language and reading a language, we assume that children who learn to read also internalize the deep structure of reading. Presumably, McLuhan has this deep structure of reading in mind when he says that the meaning of literacy has nothing to do with the content of the printed words. By "content" he means something like what Chomsky means by surface structure. For McLuhan, the deep structure of reading involves such characteristics as the static quality of the printed words, the abstraction of language from the binary process of dialogue (the dichotomy self–others), the qualities of re-

6. Segall, Campbell, and Herskovits, *The Influence of Culture on Visual Perception,* p. 10.

7. See Floyd H. Allport's theory of brain structure as consisting of interrelated loops in *Theories of Perception and the Concept of Structure.*

peatability and uniformity, and so forth. Once children have internalized this deep structure, they use it to generate behavior in activities other than reading; they exhibit, that is, the qualities of literacy that McLuhan describes in *Understanding Media*.

Although McLuhan is more concerned with the effects of literacy than with how people acquire it, passages in *Understanding Media* such as the following are consistent with these assumptions:

> It is necessary to see literacy as typographic technology, applied not only to the rationalizing of the entire procedures of production and marketing, but to law and education and city planning, as well. The principles of continuity, uniformity, and repeatability derived from print technology have, in England and America, long permeated every phase of communal life. In those areas a child learns literacy from traffic and street, from every car and toy and garment. (p. 300)

Children in the United States and Great Britain "learn literacy" by internalizing the deep structure of literacy from their immediate environment, because literate adults have generated this environment.

We learn to see and hear as we learn to speak. People blind from birth who are surgically given sight do not simply open their eyes and "see"—they have to learn to see. And just as we do not all learn to speak in the same way, i.e., in the same language, we do not all learn to see in the same way. The context of this discussion thus explains the differences in visual perception that the authors of *The Influence of Culture on Visual Perception* found between literate people and nonliterate: the two groups have internalized different paradigms for seeing. But one cannot, of course, limit this difference to seeing, for the various paradigms interact. Those who learn to read internalize and therefore generate dichotomies. Sight becomes the most important cognitive sense for them, and the imagery of sight—visual images that express the dichotomies of isolated bodies in space—comes naturally to them. In short, they exhibit the characteristics of the linear paradigm, which we can now associate with literacy. Similarly, peoples among whom literacy has had little importance retain the binary form of dialogue as a major feature of their paradigms, and thus we can associate the nonlinear paradigm with oral culture or orality. The situation of the nonlinear paradigm is complicated, of course, since it includes both true orality and the still nascent secondary or postliterate orality that the binary form of electricity has created. (Ong has quite properly warned against too readily identifying the two.)[8] In any case, the negative quality of *nonlinear* indicates that we have only a provisional understanding of the term. Having made these associations, I wish to emphasize immediately that such a general descriptive scheme cannot possibly account for the many differences that appear between one literate society and another, or between one oral society and another. Following Chomsky, I would relate such differences to surface structure, not deep structure.

As this book makes clear, I believe in the historicity of concepts and art forms. It therefore seems to me that Newton could not have articulated his theory of uniform space, which creates a dichotomy between inert space and the objects it contains and relies on visual imagery, until he, and European thought in general, had become sufficiently literate to generate such a dichotomy. When electricity made visual thought less paradigmatic, such dichotomies lost their universality. What does this mean about the truth that Newton's equations expressed adequately in 1750, but by 1950 were not sufficient to express? Another aspect of visual perception may offer a possible answer. Benjamin Whorf noticed that color words in Hopi, for example, do not match color words in English; he found that the Hopi, who have no word for purple, use the same word for purple as for brown. However, subsequent anthropological studies have found that these variations occur within limits, and not completely at random. Somehow, successful paradigms may unite arbitrary and determined features in a binary relationship in ways we cannot yet talk about.

I now wish to explicate the nonlinear paradigm in a rather different manner by discussing some criticisms of McLuhan's treatment of the relationship between media and social change. The most notorious of these, of course, is his distinction between hot and cool media, which various critics have attacked as vague and inconsistent. Naturally, McLuhan interprets the shift from the chirographic culture of the medieval manuscript to the print culture of movable type as the event that released the energy of the Renaissance. Thus the manuscript was hot during the Middle Ages—in the absence of movable type. After Gutenberg, however, it became cool—at least in comparison to print. As McLuhan himself says, "It makes all the difference whether a hot medium is used in a hot or cool culture" (p. 30), and—more specifi-

8. Walter J. Ong, S. J., *The Presence of the Word,* pp. 301–2.

cally—that "The effect of the entry of the TV image will vary from culture to culture in accordance with the existing sense ratios in each culture" (p. 45). Clearly, then, the definitions of hot and cool are not absolutely fixed. They have a meaning only in a specific historical context, which has various media that interrelate in various ways. A house in which the temperature stands at seventy degrees is also neither hot nor cool. How we perceive it when we enter depends on the weather outside.

Thus, when Donald F. Theall objects to "McLuhan's whole assumption that media affect all human beings in a similar way,"[9] he is in one sense simply wrong, for the quotations above prove that McLuhan makes no such assumption. But in a more general sense Theall is raising the issue of the very possibility of systemic thought. Humean skepticism, which in effect Theall represents here, doubts the possibility of relating any two events, objects, or concepts, and without this possibility one cannot think systematically. Rather than attempt to refute Hume here, I prefer to relate Theall's objection to the noncontinuous subset of the linear paradigm, and thereby interpret it as a typically literate response.

Christopher Ricks offers a similar, but more extreme, objection to systemic thought. McLuhan's statement, "That Hitler came into political existence at all is directly owing to radio and public-address systems" (p. 300), makes Ricks very indignant and a bit sarcastic:

> Mr. McLuhan may perhaps be right, but Hitler seems to me a subject where too serene a confidence in one's own theories can easily look unfeeling. After all, there are those of us who would have traded all of Pope Pius' words about mass media for just a word or two about the massacre of the Jews.[10]

Ricks is doing two related things here. First he is defending the use of dichotomies (in this case, Hitler–humanity in general). Second, he bases—and I use the static image deliberately—the dichotomy on a belief in the importance of isolated thoughts. Ricks wants the thought of Hitler to continue to evoke outrage in us and probably considers this the best way to prevent another outbreak of genocide. I will address this problem more specifically in Chapter 12, but for now I would like to interpret his objection as an attack on the antipsycholo-

9. Donald F. Theall, *The Medium Is The Rear View Mirror,* p. 210.
10. Christopher Ricks, "Electronic Man," in *McLuhan: Hot and Cool,* ed. Gerald Emanuel Stearn, pp. 213–14.

gism that has characterized twentieth-century systemic thought since Husserl. By definition, systemic interpretations of history attempt to deal with events as holistic processes. Moral condemnation of individuals denies those processes their holistic qualities by creating the dichotomy individual–process. In analyzing the operation of systems in history, McLuhan is, as it were, applying Hegel's dictum "Was ist, ist vernunft." (Whatever is, is rational.) Although in a nonlinear paradigm determinism does not operate in history, whatever happens in history happens in a manner that makes sense in terms of systems.

Another of McLuhan's critics, Dennis Duffy, grants that systems operate, but assumes that they operate in a mechanical fashion. Note the spatial implications of the word *located* in the following comment on McLuhan's theory of fragmentation:

> What makes it novel is that a new cause for the split has been located—the invention of movable type. The question then arises as to whether the reader is willing to grant that exterior causes come about before interior states and that the outside produces the inside world. There is no definite way of settling so basic a question. If there were, Freudians and Marxists would have blended into one another long ago. Yet somewhere a thinker must come down on one side or the other, inner or outer.[11]

Two statements in *Understanding Media* anticipate this objection. In his whimsical way, McLuhan points out that questions of pure sequence involve dichotomies: "Instead of asking which came first, the chicken or the egg, it suddenly seemed that a chicken was an egg's idea for getting more eggs" (p. 12). More explicitly, McLuhan allies himself with what Chomsky calls the "mentalism" of generative grammar:

> Stress on literacy is a distinguishing mark of areas that are striving to initiate that process of standardization that leads to visual organization of work and space. Without psychic transformation of the inner life into segmented visual terms by literacy, there cannot be the economic "take-off" that insures a continual movement of augmented production and perpetually accelerated change-and-exchange of goods and services. (p. 300)

11. Dennis Duffy, *Marshall McLuhan,* p. 29.

Just as children cannot speak until they internalize the deep structure of their parents' language, so societies cannot generate literate structures until some significant portion of its population has sufficiently internalized the deep structure of literacy so that it can generate literate patterns of behavior and literate artifacts. As my comments on Newton a few pages back indicate, I consider his theories a particularly important example of this process.

I have cited and analyzed these criticisms of McLuhan not simply to show their inaccuracy—for example, accusations about statements McLuhan did not make—but primarily in order to make a point about changes in paradigms. When a codification of a new paradigm appears, people usually perceive it in terms of the old one—and judge it as an inferior version. As the most obvious example of this, one might mention the condemnation that McLuhan's playful, epigrammatic style provoked. In conceptual terms, most of McLuhan's critics have reacted in a typically linear manner by denouncing his binary pairs, and by asserting the emotional satisfaction of using dichotomies.

I certainly do not wish to suggest in this chapter that *Understanding Media* is beyond criticism, or that one should necessarily accept all of its formulations. Any one statement of a paradigm represents one stage in its process of development. Any useful, innovative version of a paradigm has the potential to make the next version more satisfying. And Chapter 1 of this book sets out to amplify the paradigm of *Understanding Media* in just this manner.

Part IV.

The Power of the Nonlinear Paradigm
Some Harmonics of the Implosion Chorus

The image of Time brought thoughts of mortality: of human beings, facing outward like the Seasons, moving hand in hand in intricate measure: stepping slowly, methodically, sometimes a trifle awkwardly, in evolutions that take recognizable shape: or breaking into seemingly meaningless gyrations, while partners disappear only to reappear again, once more giving pattern to the spectacle: unable to control the melody, unable, perhaps, to control the steps of the dance.
—Anthony Powell

Chapter 10

Amplifications of the Nonlinear Paradigm

McLuhan surely knew that there was a good deal of rearview mirrorism in Wyndham Lewis's statement, "The artist is constantly engaged in writing a detailed history of the future because he is the only person aware of the nature of the present." Lewis is using the typical modernist image of the isolated artist here, and in the electric age, art has become much more a collective enterprise—often one that only incidentally involves writing. McLuhan himself says, for example, "Film is not really a single medium like song or the written word, but a collective art form with different individuals directing color, lighting, sound, acting, speaking" (p. 292). Naturally, the same applies to television and recording.

To make such general observations rigorous, we should probably substitute *art,* or simply *creativity,* for *artist.* The desired rigorous observation should also imply the suprapersonal quality of all systems. Thus I offer the following heuristic formulation[1]: Creativity occurs when cultural tradition interacts with the social process and manifests itself as a model of that process; the model serves as an epistemological operator for the social process.

Artistic models have an inherent incompleteness in that no one model can suffice for the entire social process. Of course that is true in general of abstractions, but the simplification of the model makes the structure of the process more readily comprehensible; and if one understands the structure of a process, one can predict its subsequent development. It is understood here that technology, as the extension of mankind, structures social processes. Moreover, both the artist's perception of the nature of technology, and the critic's articulation of

1. I borrow two terms here: the concept of art as a *model* comes from Yury Lotman, *Struktura khudozhestvennogo teksta,* pp. 18ff.; the term *epistemological operator* comes from Eugenio Donato, "The Two Languages of Criticism," in *The Languages of Criticism and the Sciences of Man,* eds. Richard Macksey and Eugenio Donato, p. 94. My use of the term differs considerably from Donato's.

perception will occur consciously and unconsciously. No matter how self-conscious either the artist or the critic may become, the binary interaction of the conscious and the unconscious will remain in effect.

Another key principle of *Understanding Media* states, "Each technology turns the previous technology into an art form." While this principle suffices for dealing in general terms with breaking points in cultural history, like the Renaissance and the twentieth century—the two periods that have principally concerned McLuhan—once one begins to work in detail on a particular period, the statement offers little help. As usual, rather than just one principle, we need two that form a binary whole. We need to say that each technology both turns the previous technology into an art form and creates a new paradigm. The early eighteenth century and the middle twentieth century—both of them periods that follow breaking points—offer classic examples of the generation of a paradigm. In the early eighteenth century, literacy began to generate the paradigm of the novel, with its emphasis on temporal succession and the individual hero. I refer the reader to Ian Watt's fine account of the process in *The Rise of the Novel.* Similarly, electricity has recently begun to generate a new paradigm in art and sculpture. In *Beyond Modern Sculpture,* Jack Burnham has discussed some of the uses of electronics in the work of various innovative sculptors.

The problems concerning media have just the opposite nature; while we have a binary pair in hot–cool, this pair has severe limitations if we wish to deal in any detail with the first half of the twentieth century. Now we find this period dominated by four media: the electric light bulb and the radio, the cinema and the automobile; and we cannot classify any of them as completely hot or completely cool. We need a scheme that will allow us to think of them as both hot and cool.

In these four media we have a pair of pairs; each unit of the pair manifests an affinity for the other, as a number of McLuhan's own analyses indicate.

Let us begin with the electric light bulb. "In a word, the message of the electric light is total change. It is pure information without any content to restrict its transforming and informing power" (p. 52). Moreover, "Electric light abolished the divisions of night and day, of inner and outer, and of the subterranean and the terrestial" (p. 126). We can easily classify as hot anything that abolishes such essential binary relationships. Furthermore, the electric light bulb (unlike the fluorescent light, a later development) emanates energy in very high definition from a single point. Yet the electric light bulb combines these hot characteristics with the cool energy of electricity and thus constitutes a hybrid medium. This same situation occurs with radio, which uses electricity to disseminate the spoken word from a single point; like print, radio abstracts language from gesture and physical presence.

In the second pair cinema has affinities with the first pair; it resembles radio in its use of point of view, and, of course, it incorporates the electric light bulb. Yet we can join cinema and the automobile because they both use the wheel—which is, oddly enough, a linear medium. Lewis Mumford noticed, in *Technics and Civilization,* that:

> Circular motion, one of the most useful and frequent attributes of a fully developed machine is, curiously, one of the least observable motions in nature.[2]

As a practical implement, the wheel extends the foot, and creates continuous sequence: "Unlike wing or fin, the wheel is linear and requires road for its completion" (p. 182).

McLuhan derives from the notion of the wheel as a linear medium this concept of cinema:

> In England the movie theater was originally called "The Bioscope," because of its visual presentation of the forms of life (from Greek *bios,* way of life). The movie, by which we roll up the real world on a spool in order to unroll it as a magic carpet of fantasy, is a spectacular wedding of the old mechanical technology and the new electric world. (p. 284)

And a similar hybrid form appears in the automobile: "It was the electric spark that enabled the gasoline engine to take over from the steam engine. The cross of electricity, the biological form, with the mechanical form was never to release a greater force" (p. 220). Both cinema and the automobile thus have the same structure in that both use the nonlinear energy of electricity to drive the linear medium of the wheel.

If these four media—the electric light and the radio, the cinema and the automobile—all constitute hybrid media, and if media struc-

2. Lewis Mumford, *Technics and Civilization,* p. 32.

ture social processes, then we can understand that they structured the horrible, beautiful rites of passage from nineteenth-century literacy to twentieth-century postliterate orality. The tensions between the hot and cool elements in these media released both destructive and creative energy at great intensity.

Chapter 11

Some Sociological and Structural Elements in Modernism

Electricity did not make the world what it is today. But no other force in the world has equaled it in shaping the structure of modern civilization. If we are to imagine a world without electricity, we must imagine a completely different society.
—Harold Sharlin, *The Making of the Electric Age,* p. 8

Patterns create meaning in a nonlinear paradigm, and even dates can cohere in patterns. Consider, for example, the following dates: Flaubert published *Madame Bovary* in book form in 1857, the same year in which Baudelaire wrote *Les Fleurs du Mal* and Wagner began *Tristan und Isolde.* Wagner began *Die Meistersinger* in 1862, the same year in which Dostoevsky published *Notes from the Underground.* Dostoevsky finished *Crime and Punishment* in 1864, and in 1865 Manet exhibited *Olympia.* The confluence of these dates suggests that during the ten years between 1855 and 1865 some of the most seminal works of modern art came into being. Or, as McLuhan puts it more generally, "As the nineteenth century heated up the mechanical and dissociative procedures of technical fragmentation, the entire attention of men turned to the associative and the corporate" (p. 39). Strictly speaking, both implosion and explosion have been occurring in Western society for the last century or so.

Since many people have written on the stylistic and technical innovations of modernist art—the denial of visual structures such as plot and perspective—it seems more useful to discuss other matters here. To study the development of modernism, as implosion, we need to know something about the development of electrical media in the nineteenth century.

Curiously enough, the use of electricity begins at the time of the demise of romanticism: "In ten inspired days during the fall of 1830, Michael Faraday discovered electromagnetic induction, found essentially all the laws that govern it, and built a working model of an electric dynamo."[1] Nevertheless, "Not until the 1880's were Faraday's theories, and the technical clues he provided, embodied in really efficient generators."[2] The half century that passed between the creation of the electromagnetic paradigm and its use in the form of generators represents a classic instance of rearview mirrorism, for very few people in the age of steam engines could understand electricity as a source of power: "Ideas about electricity moved along paths determined by the use of the mechanical model."[3]

However, the use of electricity as a communications medium developed more rapidly in the early stages. Cooke and Wheatstone, the two British inventors of the telegraph, received a patent for their device in 1837. Samuel F. B. Morse received an American patent for a telegraph in 1840, and by the 1850s both England and the United States had telegraph service in the major cities. But electricity creates a need for totality, and by 1861, the telegraph joined the East and West coasts of the United States. Moreover, Cyrus Field headed an enterprise that successfully laid the first transatlantic cable in 1866. After the telegraph (which interacted with railroads to create much hybrid energy) came the telephone, which Alexander Graham Bell successfully displayed at the Centennial Exhibition in 1876. "In 1887, the United States had almost 159,000 subscribers as compared with approximately 86,000 for the rest of the world combined."[4]

With radio, as with the electric generator, a fifty-year lag occurred between the creation of the paradigm (in this case, James Clerk Maxwell's equations in 1861), and commercial operation (1911). The radio exhibits rearview mirrorism most obviously in its original name, the *wireless*. A wireless communications medium became possible when Guglielmo Marconi had the idea of raising the transmitter on an antenna—although no known scientific principle dictated this. In December 1901, Marconi received the first transatlantic radio communication, and "In 1909 the United States passed the first law requiring wireless on passenger ships."[5]

An understanding of the reciprocal interaction of communications media and art in the nineteenth century may begin by bringing all these dates together. The crucial decade of the genesis of modern

1. Harold I. Sharlin, *The Making of the Electric Age,* p. 134.
2. Ibid.
3. Ibid., p. 74.
4. Ibid., p. 69.
5. Ibid., p. 94.

art, 1855–1865, coincides with the rise of telegraphic communications. The telephone coincides with impressionism and decadence in art, and radio coincides with cubism. Even without McLuhan's analyses of the cool structure of modern painting, one might suspect that, at the least, some relationship existed between art and electrical media, because space became a crucial issue in both. The *Baltimore Patriot* seemed to anticipate the reorganization of space in painting when it quoted some telegraph dispatches on the second day of operation of the Baltimore-Washington telegraph line in 1844, and announced, "This is indeed the annihilation of space."[6]

To put it simply, the early innovators in electricity didn't know what they were doing and could therefore do it. Morse was an artist, Cyrus Field had no technical training at all, Bell knew virtually nothing about electricity when he invented the telephone, and Marconi described himself as "an ardent amateur student of electricity."[7] Their lack of expertise became an advantage when they worked with electricity. Expertise in the nineteenth century meant literacy, and hence linear thought patterns. Significantly, the same holds for theorists. Nikolai Lobachevsky, who invented non-Euclidean geometry in 1826, taught at the University of Kazan, in central Russia, and hence had little contact with European science. Likewise, Einstein had very little to do with academic science until he achieved eminence. Einstein once said in fact, "Before I was thirty, I never met a real physicist."[8] Einstein was thirty in 1909, four years after the publication of his epochmaking paper, "The Electrodynamics of Moving Bodies" (1905).

These facts all conform to the pattern that Kuhn finds in the lives of those who bring about scientific revolutions:

> Usually . . . they are men so young or so new to the crisis-ridden field that practice has committed them less deeply than most of their contemporaries to the world view and rules determined by the old paradigm. (p. 144)

As it happens, the "crisis-ridden field" was literacy itself, and individuals whose milieu and psychology gave them less literate perceptions than others did the seminal work in electrical media. McLuhan has

6. Quoted in ibid., p. 21.
7. Quoted in ibid., p. 92.
8. Quoted in Leopold Infeld, *Albert Einstein, His Work and Its Influence on Our World,* p. 119.

said the same thing about the more specific case of twentieth-century physics: "Men in the older oral societies of middle Europe are better able to conceive the nonvisual velocities and relations of the subatomic world" (pp. 341–42). For well over a century now, the outsider has played a key role in the development of art and science. This has occurred not because being an outsider, a rebel of some kind, has an inherent value but because the outsider has internalized literacy to a lesser degree.

However, in his book on literary generations, Henri Peyre denies the validity of such reasoning: "It is our conviction that nothing, for long years to come, will arrive to elucidate significantly the mystery of the appearance of genius, even less to produce genius."[9] Given the dichotomy between mystery and mechanical causality, Peyre chooses mystery. By assuming that coherence—not determinism—characterizes history, we can understand the appearance of genius, and especially the concentration of genius in a brief period, as a release of the energy of a particular social process.

Thus, according to Peyre "generation AA," the generation born between 1875 and 1885, created modernism as an international movement. An amplified and reorganized version of Peyre's generation AA looks like this:

1875—Thomas Mann; Rainer Maria Rilke
1876—Constantin Brancusi; Raymond Duchamp-Villon; Fillippo Marinetti; Maurice de Vlaminck
1877—Raoul Dufy; Hermann Hesse; Alexei Remizov
1878—Kazimir Malevich; Carl Sandburg; Georg Kaiser
1879—E. M. Forster; Paul Klee; Francis Picabia; Wallace Stevens
1880—Guillaume Apollinaire; Andrei Bely; Ernst Bloch; Alexandr Blok; André Derain; Franz Marc; Robert Musil; Max Pechstein
1881—Bela Bartók; Jacob Epstein; Carlo Carrá; Natalya Goncharov; Mikhail Larionov; Fernand Léger; Pablo Picasso; Gino Severini
1882—Umberto Boccioni; Georges Braque; Edward Hopper; James Joyce; Wyndham Lewis; Dorothy Richardson; Igor Stravinsky; Virginia Woolf
1883—Theo van Doesburg; Franz Kafka; Anton Webern; William Carlos Williams

9. Henri Peyre, *Les générations littéraires,* pp. 173–74.

1884—Max Beckmann; Amedeo Modigliani; Karl
Schmidt-Rotluff; Sean O'Casey; Yevgeny Zamyatin
1885—Alban Berg; Robert Delaunay; Velemir Khlebnikov; D. H.
Lawrence; Ezra Pound

Even the names that are not included in this decade attest to its
importance, for there are not many of them, and they do not fall
outside it by very much. We have only to go back to 1874 for writers
such as Robert Frost and forward to 1887 to include Jean Arp, Marc
Chagall, Marcel Duchamp, Juan Gris, August Macke, and Kurt Schwit-
ters. T. S. Eliot and Georgio de Chirico were born in 1888. The last
eighty years so abound in talent and genius that since 1890 (Boris
Pasternak) and 1891 (Sergei Prokofyev), every year has witnessed the
birth of several exceptionally creative people. Furthermore, some
extraordinary innovators who did not work in the arts fall into this
period as well: C. G. Jung (1875); Albert Einstein (1879); and Walter
Gropius and John Maynard Keynes (1883).

Music and American poetry conform most completely to this
pattern of birthdates. Without Schoenberg (1874), Stravinsky, Webern, Berg, and Bartók, no one can think of the modernist sensibility in
music; Sandburg, Stevens, Williams, and Frost (1874) created what we
think of as modern American poetry. Because of the early rise of
impressionism and symbolism in France, painting and poetry in
Europe do not present as strong a case in the same way. However,
if we go back to 1871 and include Proust, we have virtually all the
crucial names in prose: Mann, Hesse, Musil, Lewis, Woolf, Richardson, Kafka, Remizov, and Lawrence. And the significant literary innovators in poetry outside of France appear here also: Rilke, Bely,
Blok, Khlebnikov, and Pound; others, such as Hugo von Hofmanns-
thal (1874), and Anna Akhmatova and T. S. Eliot (1888) come close.
In sculpture and painting we have, not an exhaustive listing, but an
extraordinary elite: Brancusi, Duchamp-Villon, Marinetti, Vlaminck,
Dufy, Malevich, Klee, Picabia, Derain, Marc, Pechstein, Carrá, Goncharov, Larionov, Léger, Picasso, Severini, Boccioni, Braque, van Doesburg, Beckmann, Modigliani, Karl Schmidt-Rotluff, Delaunay.

McLuhan's statement about men in the older oral societies of
middle Europe being better able to conceive the nonvisual velocities
and relations of the subatomic world also applies to the creation of
modernist art. In the period 1875–1885, we have a number of well-
known Central European names: Brancusi, Malevich, Goncharov, La-

rionov, Stravinsky, and Bartók. The Bauhaus, which probably brought together more creative men in one place than any other similar organization in the history of the world, was staffed to a considerable extent with Central Europeans. At the other geographical extreme, Spain and Ireland have similarly retained what Ong calls "residual orality."

This matter of residual orality explains three anomalous innovators who fall outside the period by as much as a full decade: William Butler Yeats (1865), Vasily Kandinsky (1866), and Luigi Pirandello (1867). By strict chronology, these men should not belong among modernists at all and certainly should not have done their best work in the twenties. Yeats, for example, was born in the same year as Rudyard Kipling, and Kandinsky was a year older than Bonnard. Yet Yeats published *The Tower* in 1928 at the age of sixty-three; Kandinsky did his magnificent circle paintings of the twenties, when he was in his later fifties; Pirandello wrote *Six Characters in Search of an Author* and *Henry IV* in 1921, at the age of fifty-four. They were able to produce innovative work at advanced ages, because Yeats grew up in Ireland, Kandinsky in Russia, and Pirandello in Sicily. Each responded deeply to the tribal traditions of his homeland, and each used them again and again in his work.

But people have not stayed put in modern times; we have to think not only about where they were born, but where they went, and why. Beginning with Gauguin's flight to Tahiti, artists have rejected the West geographically as well as artistically and intellectually. Between Rilke's trip to Russia and Hesse's trip to India intervened journeys of crucial importance for two modernists, Hulme and Klee. After Hulme left Cambridge without taking a degree in 1906, he spent eight months in Canada. Alun Jones has this to say about the meaning of Hulme's experience in Canada.

> Any conversion of a religious kind that he may have undergone was brought about not by reading or persuasion but by the realization, while in Canada, of man's cosmic insignificance. His faith in dogma, he always insisted, was rooted not in bigotry, but in experience, and particularly his experience of Canadian prairies. He was haunted by the vast image of space, by the huge sky and the flat, rolling grasslands reaching out to the horizons. . . . In the cold vastness of Canada he experienced the essential differences between the human and divine worlds.[10]

10. Alun Jones, *The Life and Opinions of T. E. Hulme*, p. 23.

One can readily imagine that Worringer's account of the relationship between man's fear of a chaotic universe and his creation of abstract images made an overwhelming impression on Hulme just after he returned from the plains of Saskatchewan. Eight years later, another intense, gifted young man defined himself to himself by leaving Europe. As André Gide had done in 1893, Paul Klee went to Tunisia in the spring of 1914. On 16 April 1914, he wrote in his diary:

> I now abandon work. It penetrates so deeply and so gently into me, I feel it and it gives me confidence in myself without effort. Color possesses me. I don't have to pursue it. It will possess me always, I know it. That is the meaning of this happy hour. Color and I are one. I am a painter.[11]

Klee did not merely discover an exotic landscape, but internalized a new system of nonlinear relationships. Another diary entry makes this point; as his ship approached Naples, he reminded himself not to get excited.

> For I am not undertaking an Italian journey, this must not be forgotten! I was in the East and now I must remain there. That music must not be mixed with others. The influences here are too dangerous![12]

But residual orality is not a simple matter, for three artists, André Gide, T. S. Eliot, and Thomas Mann, grew up in highly literate environments, left them as soon as they could, and never went back. Their reasons for going to Paris, London, and Munich, respectively, may serve to indicate the complexity of the sociological elements in creativity. Gide went to Paris because Paris, like other large cities, had taken fragmentation beyond the break point, at which it reversed itself. Paris offered possibilities for new forms of integration which the monolithic literacy of the provinces prevented. Eliot went to London because to an American (especially a Midwesterner), England—with her unwritten constitution, monarch, and highly ritualized government—represents an oral tradition, yet one to which a cultivated foreigner can adapt with a minimum of culture shock. As for Mann, he incorporated in his life, and expressed in his work the bifurcation in his country between the literate Protestant north of his birth and the

11. *The Diaries of Paul Klee,* ed. with an introduction by Felix Klee, p. 297.

12. Ibid., pp. 305-6.

oral, Roman Catholic south, which attracted him. This difference between northern and southern Germany appeared clearly in intellectual matters. Thus H. Stuart Hughes says that in the 1890s, "People spoke of a 'southwest German philosophy,' of a markedly anti-positivist character."[13]

Factors other than geography can exclude one from literacy. Psychological matters such as sexual preference and membership in a minority can have the same effect. Even a cursory list of creative twentieth-century homosexuals, for example, would require a great deal of space. In addition to the obvious example of Proust, such names as E. M. Forster (and practically all of Bloomsbury, many of whom were indeed bisexual), Gide, and Cocteau come to mind. Like homosexuals, Jews frequently play roles as inside–outsiders, and played a similarly disproportionate (to their percentage in the population) role in creating modernism.

The generation of 1885 interests us primarily because it created important art that embodied and expressed the growing energy of implosion. The reaction against literacy began in France, where the revolution and Napoleon had combined to institutionalize literacy earlier than in any other country. Naturally, the social process passed the breaking point and reversed itself as implosion first in France as well. An analysis of the development of implosion from Baudelaire, who found in Swedenborg assertions of the coherence that his own society lacked, through Mallarmé, in whose *Un coup de dés* (1897) literacy becomes aware of itself as such for the first time, would make a fascinating study.

One aspect of symbolism, its concern with music and musical imagery, continued to have great importance in the twentieth century. The symbolists' enthusiasm for Wagner's *Gesamtkunstwerk* constituted a first recognition of the relationship between electricity and sound, a recognition that continued in literature in Eliot's *Four Quartets,* and in Mann's interpretation of German history through music in *Doctor Faustus.* But musical themes and references constitute only one pole of a binary pair, whose other pole consists of an awareness of the decrease in importance of the eye, and of visual thought in general. As we know, Nietzsche's image of the Cyclops eye proved seminal. The Russian poet Osip Mandelstam explicated it with his characteristic passion and perspicacity:

13. H. Stuart Hughes, *Consciousness and Society,* p. 47.

The cognitive capacities of the nineteenth century stood in no relationship whatsoever to its will, its character, or its moral growth. Like the enormous eye of a Cyclops, the cognitive capacity of the nineteenth century is turned to the past and to the future. Nothing but empty and predatory sight devouring any object, any epoch, with identical greed.[14]

For Mandelstam, as for Eliot, vision had created a wasteland. The very capacity to recognize this fact derived from a contrast between the ear and the eye.

If, because of implosion, the ear began to replace the eye as the primary cognitive organ, and if each technology turns the previous technology (in this case, literacy) into an art form, we expect to find the eye used as an art form. Indeed, Gerald Eager has written an article, "The Missing Eye and the Mutilated Eye in Contemporary Art," on this very topic. Eager observes:

Special emphasis has been given to the blind eye in recent painting and sculpture—an emphasis which is seen in the repeated use of two new types of eyes in art. One type is the missing eye: the eye that has been left out of a representation of a face, leaving no indication that anything had ever been there (as though the artist did not know that such a feature existed). The other type is the mutilated eye—the eye that has been attacked in a representation of a face, leaving painted or sculptured scars (as though the artist decided to scratch out the eye that he had included at first).[15]

Both of the "new types of eyes" in art tell us the same thing, but with varying emphases. "The eye that has been left out" announces that we live in an oral age, while the mutilated eye announces that we have recently passed through a visualist age. Eager names Nathan Oliveira's *Man Walking* as an example of a work in which the artist omits the eyes altogether, and Alberto Giacometti's *Seated Man* as an example of a work in which the artist has mutilated the eyes.

Of pre-World War II works, Eager mentions de Chirico's *Two Sisters* (1915) and Picasso's *Weeping Woman* (1937) as works in

14. Osip Mandelstam, *Sobranie sochinenii, II,* p. 318. Cf. the physicist Arthur Eddington's question: "What was the world like before man limited himself to vision?" Arthur Eddington, *The Nature of the Physical World,* p. 316.

15. Gerald Eager, "The Missing and the Mutilated Eye in Contemporary Art," *Journal of Aesthetics and Art Criticism,* p. 49.

which eyes are mutilated or missing. But one could quite easily extend this list by citing only the works of Picasso. In *Les Demoiselles d'Avignon* (1907), for example, the figure in the upper right corner has a black spot for an eye cavity, as do his *Head of a Woman* (1907) and *Seated Woman* (1909). None of the other figures interact in any way. All of them have what Eager calls the "blank staring eye," as in Leon Golub's *Colossal Head*. Actually, this blank staring eye, lost in contemplation, recurs throughout modern painting.

Eager mentions another way of negating the function of the eye by closing it, as in Bernini's famous statute *St. Teresa*: "The closed sensitive eye remains aloof and constant because it is no longer affected by the external stimuli and does not now directly reflect them."[16] Intense emotion implies depth and interiority, and thus denies vision, which perceives only surfaces. (Hence, the distinction between sight and insight.) Dream states, in which we give up conscious strivings for contact with an archetypal world, form an obvious image for communicating to a world which was beginning to hear again. This fact possibly explains the importance of Henri Rousseau's *The Sleeping Gypsy* (1897) and Chagall's *The Resting Poet* (1915); one could in fact interpret the corpus of both painters' works as images of dream states. Furthermore, most of the figures in the paintings of Picasso's blue period have their eyes closed, as does the figure in *Portrait of Ambroise Vollard* (1909–1910).

But eye symbolism does not occur only in painting. Eager himself gives a striking example from the Bunuel-Dali film, *Un Chien Andalou* (1927).

> There is a sequence in which a man slices a girl's eye with a razor. This is the strongest single image in the movie, provoking screams (and sometimes sickness) in uninitiated viewers. . . .
> The destruction of the eye is reinforced by the attitudes of the man and the girl. The man does the cutting in a trance which he achieved in werewolf fashion by gazing at the moon being cut by a cloud. *The girl shows no resistance at all as the razor approaches her eye—almost as if there is a willingness on her part to be blinded.*[17]

We have here a typically startling surrealist image of the destruction of visualism inherent in all significant twentieth-century art, which

16. Ibid., p. 55.
17. Ibid., p. 51: my emphasis.

usually goes about its task more gently. But Eager mentions only this one sequence; eye symbolism also structures Eisenstein's film *Potemkin*, completed two years before *Un Chien Andalou.*

In the middle twenties, Eisenstein—like Mayakovsky—could still believe in the revolution as a triumph of the oral, tribal Russian people over the visualist czarist regime. Upon arriving in Odessa, he instantly grasped the potential of the steps to the waterfront for creating a stunning sequential image. This justly famous sequence in *Potemkin* derives its power from Eisenstein's use of the aggressive qualities of visualism in relentlessly advancing soldiers dressed in immaculate white uniforms (which should be compared to the same effect in the "psychological attack" in Vasilievs's *Chapayev,* 1934) with fixed bayonets held at the same angle. When one of them shoots a woman's eye out (Eisenstein gives us a close-up of her bloody eye socket), he does so not to destroy her vision but to destroy her self, since he identifies the eye and the self. But to understand how the Odessa steps sequence develops the use of visualism in the film as a whole, we have to return to the beginning of the film.

At the start of *Potemkin,* the discovery of maggots in the meat agitates the sailors intensely; the officers call Smirnov, the ship's doctor, who comes in and adjusts his pince-nez as he looks at the meat. Although a close-up clearly shows the maggots, Smirnov denies their existence. Thus, the first incident in the film establishes the falsity of purely visual perception. To remind the viewer of this, Eisenstein uses a close-up of Smirnov's pince-nez that catches on a piece of rigging after the sailors throw Smirnov overboard. But in addition to Smirnov, Kaluninchuk, the sailor who began the mutiny by smashing a plate (which has the inscription, "Give us this day our daily bread") also drowns. The sailors lay him out on the wharf, and Eisentein distinguishes social classes in this emotional scene (which immediately precedes the Odessa steps sequence) by the use of glasses.

The wealthy townspeople, who do not mourn Kaluninchuk, wear glasses, as does a man who makes an anti-Semitic remark. Several society ladies in frilly dresses raise their lorgnettes to look disdainfully at the corpse as they pass by. In contrast, the poor elderly women in the foreground who do mourn Kaluninchuk do not wear glasses. Thus, the Odessa steps sequence merely expresses more intensely the hostility of the visualist attitudes already present in the film: after the extraordinary tension of the long sequence, people sometimes perceive the last section, section five, as anticlimatic. This probably happens because Eisenstein switches his attention from people to the machinery of the ship, which works as a unit now that the sailors have taken over. He treats the gears, dials, and so forth as an art form very much in the manner of the futurists and Léger—but more successfully because his quick cuts impart dynamism to the action.

Unlike Eisenstein, American artists could not even temporarily believe in their country's triumph over visualism; as McLuhan said in *War and Peace in the Global Village:*

> The United States is by far the most visually organized country in the history of the world. It is the only country that was ever founded on the basis of phonetic literacy for all. All of its political and business institutions assume the ground plan of this literacy. All of its production and consumption are expressions of the same literacy: Labels and classifications for everything and everybody.[18]

As a result of the overwhelming literacy of America, implosion affected American artists rather differently from European artists. Two of the classic American novels, F. Scott Fitzgerald's *The Great Gatsby* (1925) and William Faulkner's *The Sound and the Fury* (1929), use eye symbolism in ways that make important statements about the industrial North and the rural South; they both associate the eye with railroads.

As steam-driven machines that must run on more or less straight, permanent tracks, railroads had fantastic fragmenting force in the nineteenth century, as Tolstoy noted in *Anna Karenina.* In fact, the railroad structured the major industrial metropolises of North America. By the time Fitzgerald was writing, this had long been a fait accompli; he could only record the results. In Chapter 2 of *The Great Gatsby,* the narrator, Nick Grant, goes into New York on the Long Island Railroad. He meets Tom Buchanan on the train, and Tom persuades him to get off at a local stop to meet his, Tom's, girl. Tom's mistress is married, but the three of them go into New York to spend Sunday in an apartment that Buchanan keeps for this purpose. Nick's description of the local stop deserves quotation in full:

> About halfway between West Egg and New York the motor road hastily joins the railroad and runs beside it for a quarter of a mile, so as to shrink away from a certain desolate area of

18. Marshall McLuhan and Quentin Fiore, *War and Peace in the Global Village,* p. 133.

land. This is a valley of ashes—a fantastic farm where ashes
grow like wheat into ridges and hills and grotesque gardens,
where ashes take the forms of houses and chimneys and rising
smoke and, finally, with a transcendent effort, of men who
move dimly and already crumbling through the powdery air.
Occasionally a line of gray cars crawls along an invisible track,
gives out a ghastly creak, and comes to rest, and immediately
the ash-gray men swarm up with leaden spades and stir up an
impenetrable cloud, which screens their obscure operations
from your sight.

But above the gray land and the spasms of bleak dust
which drift endlessly over it, you perceive, after a moment, the
eyes of Doctor T. J. Eckleburg. The eyes of Doctor T. J.
Eckleburg are blue and gigantic—their retinas are one yard high.
They look out of no face, but, instead, from a pair of enormous
yellow spectacles which pass over a non-existent nose.
Evidently some wild wag of an oculist set them there to fatten
his practice in the borough of Queens, and then sank down
himself into eternal blindness, or forgot them and moved away.
But his eyes, dimmed a little by many paintless days under sun
and rain, brood on over the solemn dumping ground.

The valley of ashes is bounded on one side by a small foul
river, and, when the drawbridge is up to let barges through, the
passengers on waiting trains can stare at the dismal scene for as
long as half an hour. There is always a halt here of at least a
minute, and it was because of this that I first met Tom
Buchanan's mistress.[19]

Fitzgerald has created here a dream image that expresses deadness
and isolation in three respects: (1) the false, cynical relationship between Buchanan and his mistress, which typifies the other relationships in the novel; (2) the linear quality of the railroad itself, which
deprives its passengers of spontaneity of movement and of any immediate relationship to a natural environment; and finally (3) visualism,
which implies all the others in various ways and subsumes them.
Historically, we can associate the railroad with industrialization,
which produced the slag heap, and thus with the wealth that created
estates such as the one in which Gatsby himself lives. But the dissociation of the animate and the inanimate, which made industrialization
possible, also made meaningful human relationships in depth difficult
at best. On that Sunday in New York, Tom breaks Mrs. Wilson's nose,

19. F. Scott Fitzgerald, *The Great Gatsby,* pp. 23–24.

and Daisy cannot tell Tom that she has never loved him. Jay Gatsby accidentally runs over Mrs. Wilson with his car along the road next to the ash heap. The narrator signals Gatsby's literacy by telling us that when he was growing up as Jimmy Gatz, he had made a schedule in which he had devoted every waking minute to some useful activity, as literate people do. But he becomes too intensely visual, and Daisy breaks down at the sight of his collection of shirts.

The contrast between the oral Faulkner and the literate Fitzgerald appears unmistakably in their use of language; after Faulkner's overwhelming ability to create beauty in both dense, polysyllabic narrative commentary and in black dialect, Fitzgerald's language seems to have a range of about two notes. When people speak of Faulkner's concern with the dissolution of Southern society, they really mean his reaction to the fragmentation that followed as an aftermath of the Civil War. Thus, when he describes the rise of the Snopes family in his trilogy, *The Hamlet, The Mansion,* and *The Town,* he is tracing the rise of the visual values they represent.

Faulkner takes up the theme of fragmentation in his first major work, *The Sound and the Fury.* In the appendix he wrote for *The Portable Faulkner,* he characterized Jason Compson as "The first sane Compson since before Culloden and (a childless bachelor) hence the last. Logical rational contained. . . ."[20] In other words, Jason has lost his patrimony of aristocracy by accepting literacy and has paid for it at the price of sterility. He pays in another, less metaphorical way as well; on Easter Sunday, 8 April 1928, his niece Quentin who lives in his house breaks into his room, steals seven thousand dollars (four thousand of which he had in effect stolen from her), and runs off with a pitchman in a traveling circus. Jason drives to the next town, to the circus train, to find them, but the manager assures him that the two have gone.

> "Keep going," the other said. He led Jason on around the corner of the station, to the empty platform where an express truck stood, where grass grew rigidly in a plot bordered with rigid flowers and a sign in electric lights; Keep your eye on Mottson, the gap filled by an eye with an electric pupil. The man released him. "Now," he said, "You get on out of here and stay out. What were you trying to do, commit suicide?"[21]

20. William Faulkner, *The Portable Faulkner,* ed. Malcolm Cowley, p. 750.
21. William Faulkner, *The Sound and the Fury,* p. 274.

In the only instance that I have found in any of Faulkner's books, he inserted a drawing of an eye on the manuscript page with this passage. The moment rather resembles a Joycean epiphany in reverse. Like the same kind of sign near the railroad tracks in *The Great Gatsby,* Mottson's sign speaks of the alienation of visualism; but Faulkner uses it with greater force. The difference between Jason and Fitzgerald's other characters is that he realizes he cannot struggle against the forces of fragmentation; they have defeated him.

Not all the images that artists created in order to express the new orality were musical in nature. Archetypal images represent psychic, as opposed to perceptual, integration and appear very frequently in modernism. Of these, I will mention the three that speak most eloquently: the horse, the fish, and the circle.

Jung interprets the horse as a symbol of the libido, of the total life force; hence the importance of the man on horseback: "The hero and his horse seem to symbolize the idea of man and the subordinate sphere of animal instinct."[22] Once we know this, we can understand the importance of Will Grohmann's statement that "Until 1912 horses and riders occur in almost all of Kandinsky's works."[23] Kandinsky took particular interest in the figure of St. George, whom Russian icons traditionally depict as a man on horseback slaying a dragon. Pasternak used the figure of St. George in the same way, but more explicitly, in *Doctor Zhivago* (1957), for he uses Yury Zhivago—the name *Yury* is a Russian variation of *George*—as a Christ figure who will bring salvation. We have something of this in Kandinsky's horses and riders, which begin, of course, with *Blaue Reiter.*[24] In sculpture, Marino Marini's near obsession with the figure of a rider on a horse also expresses this sense of new strength.

Of the image of the fish Jung says:

> The fish in dreams occasionally signifies the unborn child, because the child before its birth lives in the water like a fish; similarly, when the sun sinks into the sea, it becomes child and fish at once. The fish is therefore a symbol of renewal and rebirth.[25]

22. Carl G. Jung, *Symbols of Transformation,* p. 275.
23. Will Grohmann, *Wassily Kandinsky,* p. 112.
24. After I had written these lines, I learned that Kandinsky himself had thought of his work in virtually identical terms; see Rose-Carol Washton, "Wassily Kandinsky: Painting and Theory, 1908–1913."
25. Jung, *Symbols of Transformation,* p. 198.

The image of the fish surely has exactly this meaning in the dreamlike paintings by Paul Klee, whose work constantly invites Jungian interpretation. Klee, who liked to visit aquariums and who kept a box of fish and plant forms in his studio, painted a number of works that have archetypal fish, such as *Fish Magic* (1925); *The Golden Fish* (1925); *Around the Fish* (1926); and *Underwater Garden* (1939).

Although no other painter of comparable stature seems to have used the fish as often as Klee, we find a number of related images in the work of other artists. Chagall's ubiquitous cows, which help to create the discontinuous space of his paintings, may suggest fertility and birth, as do Brancusi's egg shapes, and Henry Moore's sculptures dealing with the theme of motherhood. Now the fish gains much of its significance from the fact that it lives in the water, whose depths provide an obvious image for the unconscious. We can thus associate it with Picasso's Minotaur, of which William S. Rubin says:

> His fascination with this ancient hybrid monster accorded with the growing interest in French intellectual circles in the psychoanalytical interpretation of myth. The labyrinth—the recesses of the mind—contains at its center the Minotaur, symbol of irrational impulses. Theseus, slayer of the beast, thus symbolizes the conscious mind threading its way into its unknown regions and emerging again by virtue of intelligence, that is, self-knowledge—a paradigmatic schema for the Surrealist drama, as indeed, for the process of psychoanalysis.[26]

The hybrid nature of the Minotaur—half-man, half-beast—also corresponds to the union of man and horse that Kandinsky liked so much. And Kandinsky seems to have used more consciously than anyone else the consummate image of totality, the circle, which he characterized in 1930 as "the synthesis of the greatest oppositions."[27] Kandinsky did not begin the use of the circle, of course. It seems to have arisen in the works of the artists associated with orphism: Robert Delaunay and František Kupka. Thus, we have Delaunay's *Circle Forms* (1912–1913), *Homage to Bleriot* (1914), and *Portugese Woman* (1916), Kupka also used the motif in numerous paintings, such as *Circle* (1911).

Finally, the conflict between literacy and orality, between the hot and cool elements of the media that structured the modernist period,

26. William S. Rubin, *Dada, Surrealism and Their Heritage,* p. 127
27. Quoted in Grohmann, *Wassily Kandinsky,* p. 187.

released destructive as well as creative energy. The modernists sensed this impending destruction and expressed it in their works by using familiar images. Picasso turned the bomb that fell on a small Spanish town into the more general, and more powerful, image of the light bulb, which has a destructive effect on all the figures in *Guernica* (1937), especially the horse. His *Fishermen of Antibes* (1939) portrays brutish figures who spear fish with tritons, and thus resembles Klee's *Scene from the Comic-Fantastic Opera "The Seafarer"* (1936). Likewise, lines often cut the circles in Kandinsky's work as well as in those of his fellow countrymen, Lazar Lissitsky and Alexandr Rodchenko. Klee's feeling in 1914 that "I have long had this war inside me"[28] refers to more than World War I. It refers to the conflict between linear and nonlinear elements of the electrical world, a conflict with social forms we may define as linear tribalism and tribal linearity.

28. Klee, *The Diaries of Paul Klee,* p. 313.

Chapter 12

Linear Tribalism

McLuhan's comment, "Speed-up creates what some economists refer to as a center-margin structure" (p. 91), provides a way of understanding some of the major political processes in the history of Western society. By "center-margin structure," McLuhan means any structure—social, political, or economic—in which people exert control at a distance; center-margin structures typically come into being by breaking down autonomous institutions in the areas they wish to control. For example, literacy in seventeenth-century France speeded up the political process sufficiently so that Louis XIV could weaken the semiautonomous units of local government and centralize the power of the monarchy over them. By using literacy to exert power at a distance, he created the center-margin structure that has characterized much of French life since the seventeenth century and that has made France an abundant source of literate forms.

Although this process did not take place without violence, it progressed slowly enough that its release of energy could produce what the French like to call "le grand siécle" in literature—the age of Racine and Molière.[1] Just as the architectural expression of this centralization of power in Versailles gave rise to numerous imitations as literacy began to fragment the Western world more and more completely in the eighteenth century, so many of the political processes in Western society resemble those that culminated in the reign of Louis XIV. In the twentieth century, electricity has greatly speeded up the centralization of power, and I am going to consider some patterns of this process in Europe and the United States. But first I want to introduce certain basic concepts.

McLuhan sets up a helpful opposition in his chapter "Radio: The Tribal Drum":

1. I am adapting here Lucien Goldmann's analysis of the relationship between the centralization of power and literature in seventeenth-century France in *The Hidden God*.

> Highly literate societies, that have long subordinated family life
> to individualist stress in business or politics, have managed to
> absorb and to neutralize the radio implosion without revolution.
> Not so, those communities that have had only brief or
> superficial experience of literacy. For them, radio is utterly
> explosive. (p. 300)

Since the effect of any medium depends on the nature of the society in which it appears, the United States and Russia—to take the two extreme examples—have differed greatly in their reaction to electricity in the twentieth century, and they have differed in a way that makes sense in terms of their experience of literacy. Some statistics will make apparent the differences between the processes of adaptation to electricity in the two countries.

By 1900 in the United States, 89.3 per cent of the population could read and write; by 1940, a generation later, the figure had increased to 97.1 per cent.[2] In contrast, the percentage of literate persons in the population of Russia between the ages of nine and forty-nine in 1897 stood at 39.1 per cent. Many of these people probably had illiterate parents, and the percentage would certainly have decreased if the figures had included older people. By 1939, however, the figure stood at 95.1 per cent.[3] That is, within a single generation literacy in Russia increased by 143.2 per cent while it increased by only 8.7 per cent in the United States. While electricity restructured the United States in a disruptive way, it arrived simultaneously with literacy in Russia, and the combination fragmented Russian society to an unprecedented degree. The institutionalized fragmentation of the United States produced a number of partially realized tribal structures. As McLuhan quips about the John Birch Society, literate people became "tribally dedicated to opposing the tribal" (p. 51). Because of its incompleteness and inconsistency, I will call this phenomenon *tribal linearity*.

I will use the term *linear tribalism* to refer to the use of literacy in a tribal manner, which resulted from the appearance of hybrid media in oral societies in Central and Eastern Europe. Since it takes several generations for a society to acquire a strongly visual organization, the Russians, who became literate (in the technical sense of the

2. These statistics come from *Progress of Literacy in Various Countries,* p. 150.
3. These statistics come from the article by George Dennis, in *McGraw-Hill Encyclopedia of Russia and the Soviet Union,* p. 152.

word) within a single generation, used literacy in a tribal manner to create linear tribalism. McLuhan says: "For the Russian, especially, it is easy to approach any situation structurally, which is to say, sculpturally" (p. 289). Thus when Russians became literate at such an astonishing rate, they used literacy in a particularly pure way.

When literacy fragments a tribal society, the first major dichotomy that appears is society–self. As literacy centralizes power, society —typically in some form of nationalism—becomes the more important half of the dichotomy: a visual form of the tribe. Tribal people find it difficult to achieve the Westerner's self-assertion, a psychological state that usually appears at a relatively advanced stage of fragmentation. When electricity appeared in Eastern Europe, it created the dichotomy society–self as a form of the center–margin dichotomy. It thereby greatly increased the tensions that literacy, in the form of the railroad and nascent industrialization, had already created. Thus, the tension that always exists between the two halves of a dichotomy became so great that the center tried to annihilate the margin and make everything the center. In this process, the center tends to destroy itself as well as the margin, something that in fact happened with Hitler and Mussolini, and very nearly with Stalin. To understand this process in greater detail we need to analyze the structural elements of linear tribalism.

Daniel Lerner begins *The Passing of Traditional Society,* a sensitive analysis of fragmentation, with an instructive chapter that he calls "The Grocer and the Chief: A Parable." Lerner's parable contrasts two men in the Turkish village of Balgat. The chief presents native revivalism, the attempt to defend tribal ways, and the grocer represents the attempt to reject them for literate values. The grocer interests us here, for he reported what Lerner calls "an abiding image of how his fantasy world might look." This "abiding image" came from a hybrid medium:

> It was in a movie that he had first glimpsed what a real grocery store could be like—"with walls made of iron sheets, top to floor and side to side, and on them standing myriads of round boxes, clean and all the same dressed, like soldiers in a great parade."[4]

4. Daniel Lerner, *The Passing of Traditional Society,* pp. 24–25.

"Clean, and all the same dressed, like soldiers in a great parade." The literate values of cleanliness, uniformity, and repeatability—with their militaristic, aggressive implications—have immense prestige for the recently fragmented person. These values informed totalitarianism, and we thus expect to find people for whom the pure forms of literacy have great prestige at the head of totalitarian movements.

As a way of subsuming individuals into the general process of fragmentation, I wish to analyze the famous dictators of Russia, Germany, and Italy in terms of literacy by using what I shall call "the three-generations hypothesis." This hypothesis assumes that when an individual becomes historically important in fragmentation, the life of his grandfather gives a key to his own career. The analysis begins with some facts about Stalin, Hitler, and Mussolini.

Stalin:

Perhaps in 1875, perhaps a year or two before, a young Caucasian, Vissarion Ivanovich (son of Ivan) Djugashvili, set out from the village of Didi-Lilo, near Tiflis, the capital of the Caucasus, to settle in the little Georgian country town of Gori. There he started a small shoemaker's business. Vissarion Djugashvili was the son of Georgian peasants who only ten years before had still been serfs. He himself had been born a chattel slave to some Georgian landlord. Had he remained so for the rest of his life, he would never have been free to leave his native village and become an independent artisan. Certainly none of his forefathers could have done anything of the sort. They had been tied to the soil, and at best they could pass only from the hands of one landlord to those of another.[5]

Mussolini:

Prominent among Bakunin's admirers and followers was Alessandro Mussolini, Benito's father. Alessandro came from a family of peasants who for generations had lived and toiled on their own bit of land until Alessandro's father, who did not like hard work, sold his property and wasted its proceeds after settling in Predappio. From his father Alessandro inherited the soul, looks, and manner of a peasant, but he was not one; he did not return to the land and, instead, became an apprentice to a smith.[6]

5. Isaac Deutscher, *Stalin: A Political Biography,* p. 1.
6. Laura Fermi, *Mussolini,* p. 7.

Hitler:

> Johann Georg Hiedler, Adolf's grandfather, was a wandering
> miller, plying his trade in one village after another in Lower
> Austria. . . . Alois Schickelgruber (Hitler's father) first learned the
> trade of shoemaker in the village of Spital, but being restless,
> like his father, he soon set out to make his fortune in Vienna. At
> eighteen he joined the border police in the Austrian customs
> service near Salzburg, and on being promoted to the customs
> service itself nine years later he married Anna Glasl-Hoerer.[7]

Like Napoleon, Hitler and Stalin were born in a country to the south
of, and more oral than, the country they were to rule; their strong
accents marked them as foreigners all their lives. In this, as in other
respects, Mussolini varies the pattern slightly, since he was born in the
Romagna section of northern Italy. But Laura Fermi calls Romagna "a
land of restlessness and rebellion, once called the Sicily of continental
Italy."[8]

The grandfathers of the three men possessed a very minimal
literacy at best; Stalin's grandfather was almost surely illiterate. Thus,
the pattern takes the following form: The violence and destruction of
each dictator's reign varies inversely with the literacy of his grandfather: the more oral the grandfather, the greater the violence when the
grandson began to use literacy. The dictator's father moved from the
land to the town. Continuing the fragmentation, Stalin's and Hitler's
fathers put pressure on them to achieve the social mobility that literacy
makes possible. Stalin's father did this by repeated beatings, in which
he vented his frustration over his own lack of success. Hitler's father
tried to force him to become that most literate of beings, a bureaucrat,
and Hitler expressed his reaction to this pressure in *Mein Kampf*.

> I did not want to become a civil servant, no, and again no. All
> attempts on my father's part to inspire me with love or pleasure
> in this profession by stories from his own life accomplished the
> exact opposite. I . . . grew sick to my stomach at the thought of
> sitting in an office, deprived of my liberty; ceasing to be the
> master of my own time and being compelled to force the
> content of my whole life into paper forms that had to be filled
> out.[9]

7. William L. Shirer, *The Rise and Fall of the Third Reich,* pp. 7–8.
8. Fermi, *Mussolini,* p. 7.
9. Quoted in Shirer, *The Rise and Fall of the Third Reich,* p. 11.

This extreme reaction against literacy helps to explain the peculiar evolution of linear tribalism.

The evolution of linear tribalism (and possibly of all mass movements in the twentieth century) consists of two stages, one for each of its elements. In Italy, Germany, and Russia, linear tribalism began as a strongly tribal movement that bore a label referring to some sort of socialism and thus had an intense appeal in oral countries. Once in power, however, the movement began to use its literate elements to bring about intense centralization. (The god that failed was tribalism, and it failed because those who believed in it ignored the intensification of literacy by electricity.) The centralization first took the form of purges of those members who wished to carry out tribal programs, and thus those who believed in the Party, a group image, and not the isolated Leader.

The reversals in Italy, Germany, and Russia took place roughly in the decade 1925–1935. In Italy, the purge followed the murder of one Giacomo Matteoti in 1924, with this result:

> With Mussolini's encouragement, Turati purged and devitalized the Party so thoroughly that it came to be regarded merely as a convenient means of securing a job or gaining promotion. Of the vague and somewhat crude dynamic idealism of the first squadristi it contained not a jot.[10]

In Germany, Ernst Roehm's brownshirted SA corresponded to Mussolini's squadristi in that both groups had done the street fighting and terroristic activities in the movement's early days; and Hitler purged Roehm and the SA in June 1934, shortly after he became chancellor. In Russia, the purges lasted much longer and destroyed many more people than in Italy or Germany because the Bolshevik party already had a relatively long and complicated history by 1925, and because the centralization of power occurred more completely, i.e., in a purer form, in the Soviet Union.

When Lenin died in 1924, a number of men had belonged to the Party longer than Stalin, and had as good a claim to leadership as he did. The very existence of these men—*totally apart from their own beliefs and ambitions*—prevented the centralization of power. Before total centralization could occur, they had to die. Thus, Stalin drove Trotsky, his primary rival, out of the Soviet Union in 1929, and had

10. A. James Gregor, *The Ideology of Fascism,* p. 56.

him murdered in 1940, just as Hitler had Georg Strasser, the one Nazi whose personality and ability made him a potential rival for power, killed during the purge of the SA in 1934. Significantly, Trotsky and Strasser wished to emphasize the genuinely socialist, genuinely revolutionary (in the economic sense) aspects of the party's program.

In Russia, the purge had to include the army because the army had kept the party in power during the civil war. Marshal Mikhail Tukhachevsky, one of Stalin's best-known victims in the purges of the army in 1937–1938, had distinguished himself as a *Wunderkind* general in the civil war and in the war with Poland while only in his twenties. His prestige and ability—once again, totally apart from his conscious thoughts and actions—made him an obstacle to centralization. The purges in Russia transformed the nature of the Bolshevik party, and tended to minimize the differences that had existed between the Bolshevik and Nazi parties in the twenties.

It is in the denial of nonliterate, nonvisual values that we find the greatest similarities between the regimes of Hitler and Stalin. Both men understood that they needed the concept of uniform space in order to exert power at a distance, and that representational painting expressed that concept. As Helmut Lehmann-Haupt puts it in *Art Under a Dictatorship,* "Like the Nazis in general, and Adolph Hitler especially, Marx considered classical art 'the standard and model beyond attainment.' "[11] Lehmann-Haupt also recalls that in November 1947, when one Lieutenant-Colonel Dymschitz (who later became a well-known government spokesman) delivered a speech about the Soviet concept of art, the audience unanimously reacted: "Exactly like the Nazis—from the ideas down to the wording."[12]

For the newly literate sensibility of linear tribalism, the manifestations of fragmentation in Greek and Renaissance art held a great attraction. In Worringer's terms, such art communicated the total control over nature that linear tribalism believes it possessed. But the tribal qualities of linear tribalism demanded the total integration of art into society. For the tribal man, art constitutes cognition of the whole. Linear tribalism demanded, and got, art that served as cognition of a linear society in which all power flows from the center. Since the

11. Helmut Lehmann-Haupt, *Art Under a Dictatorship,* p. 9. Cf. Albert Speer, "Hitler believed that the culture of the Greeks had reached the peak of perfection in every field." Albert Speer, *Inside the Third Reich,* p. 96.
12. Lehmann-Haupt, *Art Under a Dictatorship,* p. 201.

centralization of power ultimately means the centralization of cognition, and hence the denial of empiricism, the actual existence of such a society has little relevance. Thus socialist realism and avant-garde modernism share an oddly similar detachment from an empirically verifiable reality; both purport to deal with what will be but what is not yet. (Socialist realism and modernism represent the two halves of a dichotomy that post-modernism is attempting to resolve.) Logically, then, there arose the necessity to destroy that art which gave cognition of decentralization and implosion—modernism.[13]

As one would expect from a social structure that rejected modernism, linear tribalism rejected Einsteinian physics as well. Einsteinian physics denies both the visual values that seem so prestigious to newly fragmented people and the determinism that linear tribalism used. Thus, the Nazis concluded, "The Jew prefers pure speculation to experimental observation of nature."[14] That is to say, Jews have nonvisual values, and in linear tribalism that makes anyone inferior. (One can readily understand their rationale for concluding this, since German Jews like Einstein had done so much to deny visual values.) Sincere visualists in Germany and Russia made successful careers out of denouncing Einstein—just as scientists in other parts of the world were doing. For example, one Phillip Lenard, a distinguished experimentalist who simply could not understand a nonvisual world, wrote an attack on Einstein that became well known.

> Lenard . . . rejected Einstein's work *because it could not present a mechanical model of optical events.* Soon after its publication in 1922, Lenard's book was translated into Russian with an introduction by Timiryasev.[15]

The physicist to whom Einstein's biographer refers here attacked relativity theory with equal vigor in the Soviet Union. After the party understood the military potential of nuclear physics, it became admis-

13. Although the Russians like to cite the radical nineteenth-century critics like Nikolai Chernyshevsky and Aleksandr Dobroliubov as theoreticians of socialist realism, the art critic Vladimir Stasov (1824–1906) seems a more appropriate choice. A true visualist, Stasov disliked impressionism because he considered it necessary to be able to determine the national origin of a painting by looking at it. On Stasov, see Michael Curran, "Vladimir Stasov and the Development of Russian National Art: 1851–1910."

14. Quoted in Phillip Frank, *Einstein, His Life and Times,* p. 251.

15. Ibid., p. 259. My emphasis.

sable in schools, but the fact of the essential incompatability of Marx-ism–Leninism with relativity theory remains.[16]

The very success of centralization posed difficulties, because of what Lewis Mumford calls "the paradox of power":

> Centralized political power takes its origins from the sheer force and capability of a dominant personality; it reaches its negation when all these attributes and energies are absorbed by an official mechanism, whereby the original power is conveyed to distant points through bureaucratic and military organization.[17]

Mumford was thinking of Louis XIV when he wrote these words, but they also define the problematic role of bureaucracy in totalitarianism. Since an efficient bureaucracy must have the power to make at least some decisions and carry them out, its existence threatens the leader, just as the existence of party members of long standing like Lev Kamenev and generals like Tukhachevsky threatened Stalin. The tribal chieftain cannot allow this, and he thus institutes various means (in addition to purges) of limiting the power of the bureaucracy, and thus the power of his own government—which centralization of power presumably increases.

From books by insiders such as *Hitler* by Otto Diedrich, the press chief of the Reich; *Inside the Third Reich* by Albert Speer; and Khrushchev's memoirs, we now know enough about the day-to-day operations of totalitarianism to understand that, aside from the deliberate cruelties, many of the horrors of totalitarianism arose from the leader's usually successful attempts to destroy the autonomy of all administrative structures. The simplest, and thus the most common, way of doing this was to appoint incompetent toadies, and defend them from all criticism. As a narrative comment in Solzhenitsyn's *The First Circle* puts it, Stalin resembled King Midas; everything he touched turned not to gold, but to mediocrity. To demonstrate talent and integrity meant to show oneself as capable of resisting centralization and thus to act as an obstacle to it. Incompetent generalship alone cost the Russians millions of lives in World War II, and the Party's emphasis on retaining central control continues to plague the Russian economy.

The tension between the necessity to centralize power and the

16. See S. Müller-Markus, "Einstein and Soviet Philosophy," *Studies in Soviet Thought,* p. 81.
17. Lewis Mumford, *The City in History,* p. 391.

necessity of fragmenting it in a bureaucracy seems ubiquitous in linear tribalism. Diedrich, who knew nothing of comparable conditions in Russia, says, "In the twelve years of his rule Hitler created in the political leadership of Germany the greatest confusion that has ever existed in a civilized state."[18] The tribal chieftain needed to play his subordinates off against each other, to create overlapping chains of command, and to give often contradictory orders. Because of the similarity of the operative forces, therefore, the official routines of the inner circles in Germany and Russia coincide down to the most minute details. Hitler and Stalin forced their subordinates to attend long, boring dinners while urgent business went unattended. The leaders watched closely for the only thing that mattered to them—signs of disloyalty in their exhausted, drunken guests. In fact, Stalin and Hitler arranged for themselves a comfortable, leisurely bourgeois life. Both not only liked long dinners, but they also showed a natural interest in a hybrid medium such as cinema, in which linear tribalism created its only aesthetic successes.

Although the oral qualities of Germany and Russia prove crucial in distinguishing these countries from France, England, and the United States, once the analysis concentrates on the comparison of Germany and Russia alone, this distinction becomes irrelevant, for it has no autonomous existence. In order to elicit other structures, one can use another distinction that has equal validity: a distinction between Germany as a relatively more literate country,[19] and Russia as a relatively less literate country.

This distinction appears, for example, in the leaders' concept of their own capacities. Stalin presented himself as an extremely cool Oriental wise man, and therefore an attractive figure in a tense era of hot fragmentation. He rarely appeared in public but inspired the people through his wisdom—not merely on the history of the Party, but on linguistics and other subjects as well. Hitler, on the other hand, had a much hotter image. According to Speer, he allowed a certain fragmentation of his power by often giving in to technical experts, and he trusted Speer himself. (Stalin would have purged such a gifted man.) Possessed of a considerably more romantic sensibility than Stalin, he

18. Otto Diedrich, *Hitler,* p. 113.

19. The dichotomy between the literate north of Germany and the oral south makes any analysis of Germany complicated. The Nazi party drew its membership primarily from the oral south, from Bavaria, but still had a certain association with the industrialists of the literate north, who supported it.

considered himself a master builder. He took an active role in creating a distinct architectural style, which corresponds in its cognitive structure to that of the first major period of fragmentation in the West. In its uniform, high-definition ornateness,[20] the architecture of linear tribalism attempted to overwhelm the individual with a sense of the omnipotence of the state and of the ruler, just as Versailles had done.

In *The City in History,* Mumford tells us, "The avenue is the most important symbol and the main fact about the Baroque city."[21] Mumford's comment helps us to interpret the following scene from Speer's chapter on "Our Empire Style," which deals with Hitler's projected plans for rebuilding Berlin.

> Hitler was particularly excited over a large model of the grand avenue on the scale of 1:1000. He loved to "enter his avenue" at various points and take measure of the future effect. For example, he assumed the point of view of a traveller emerging from the south station or admired the great hall as it looked from the heart of the avenue. To do so, he bent down, almost kneeling, his eye an inch or so above the level of the model, in order to have the right perspective, and while looking he spoke with unusual vivacity. These were the rare times when he relaxed his usual stiffness.[22]

This incident tells us as much about the visualism of the Nazi regime as the fact that Himmler chose members of the SS from photographs. As Mumford says, the avenue served military purposes not only because artillery could command it easily but also because of the displays of military strength which it makes possible: "The esthetic effect of the regular ranks and the straight line of soldiers greatly contributes to the display of power, and a regiment moving thus gives the impression that it would break through a solid wall without losing a beat."[23] Mumford

20. Cf. Fritz Baumgart: "In fact, Behrens and a number of other . . . architects deliberately took up Classicism again because they recognized in it the beginnings of a new approach to architecture. When the Communist and National-Socialist dictatorships returned to the same source later, they were not stepping out of the mainstream of architectural development, but at the same time they did not introduce this kind of creative metamorphosis. In fact, they simply imitated, and in doing so they descended to the level of the democratic-capitalist middle-classes of the second half of the nineteenth century whom they hated so much" (Fritz Baumgart, *A History of Architectural Styles,* p. 283).

21. Mumford, *The City in History,* p. 367.
22. Speer, *Inside the Third Reich,* p. 133.
23. Mumford, *The City in History,* p. 367.

would call the goose step of the Nazis a baroque invention, of course. Not coincidentally, the soldiers who make up the honor guard at Lenin's Tomb in Red Square do a goose step to and from their barracks. The contradiction between the hot, linear goose step (as well as the May Day parade of weapons) and the cool, wrap-around space of Red Square makes the hybrid nature of linear tribalism obvious even to the casual observer. In Germany, the manner in which the cool, tribal party rallies implied the hot, fragmented concentration camps expressed the same contradiction.

The distinction between the Germans as relatively hot and the Russians as relatively cool also makes sense of the two countries' use of torture and concentration camps. To begin, one should keep in mind that only literate people can operate concentration camps—the ultimate form of fragmentation—for the administrators and guards constantly act without reacting to others. Moreover, literacy creates the dichotomy center–margin, which generates the camps in the first place. Through concentration camps, the center tries to destroy the margin, on which its existence depends.

The Germans made relatively careful distinctions as to who they shipped to the camps. People who were not Jews, Jewish sympathizers, or political activists could feel relatively free from arrest. In contrast to the Russian situation, the relatively greater openness of Germany in the thirties made it possible for a relatively larger number of artists and scientists to escape. The camps themselves sometimes had the appearance of a stage setting, as in the famous painted clock on the railroad station at Auschwitz. In them, torture and mass murder expressed the need for *Lebensraum,* "a claustrophobia, engendered by radio implosion and compression of space" (p. 301). Finally, in a world that continued to experience implosion at a rapid rate after 1945, the hot Nazis have seemed like the stuff of nightmares to many —especially since we have hot movies of the liberation of some of the death camps and hot photographs of them.

The Russian reaction to implosion differed markedly from the German. The most important difference is that no one could ever feel really free from arrest. To be sure, arrests in the twenties concentrated on such obvious enemies as priests and members of dissident political parties, and subsequently on members of ethnic minorities such as Jews, Chircassians, Volga Germans, and Crimean Tartars. But the Russians generally thought of any individual as constituting as much of a threat to centralization of power as any other individual. The center thus acted perfectly consistently when it sent out orders to a regional office for the arrest of, say, five thousand enemies of the people. Precisely in the image of industrialization and literacy, people became interchangeable: any enemy of the people served as well as any other.

Interrogation consequently played a far more important role in Russia than in Germany. While Russian interrogators certainly enjoyed hearing their prisoners scream as much as their German counterparts, torture in Russia almost always had as its direct purpose the extraction of a confession, since the Russians repeated with millions of ordinary people the pattern of the purge trials. To force people to confess to crimes they could not possibly have committed is to extend the power of the center over the margin in a very explicit way. The Russians did not need to use ovens and gas chambers because they had the space of Siberia and Central Asia in which they could work people to death; in these bleak, uninhabited, and virtually uninhabitable areas, concentration camps had a rough-hewn quality that characterizes much of linear tribalism in Russia. Although it is widely accepted that the Russians probably killed more people than the Nazis, people in the West have had relatively little awareness of this because the Russians have successfully controlled the media. We have no movies of Soviet concentration camps or pictures of Soviet torture chambers.

Just as one cannot understand Stalin without reference to his grandfather's illiteracy, so one cannot understand the problem of the centralization of power in the Soviet Union without reference to the manner in which this problem has recurred through Russian history. From the very beginnings of Kievan Rus' the lack of natural defenses on the plains of what became Russia and the Ukraine, and the presence of powerful enemies on the east, west, and south, forced the Eastern Slavs to centralize power in the prince, who acted primarily as a military leader. In a complex manner that Michael Cherniavsky has set forth in his book *Tsar and People,* there arose a belief in the leader's inherent sanctity, and this belief effectively checked the growth of an efficient bureaucracy.

A study of Russian history also helps one to understand the lack of uniformity in historical development. While this tension between the military necessity of centralizing power and the quasi-religious fear of institutionalizing it in a bureaucracy has structured much of Russian history, it has operated more strongly at some times than at others. While fragmentation, like implosion, occurs continuously, pulses occur during which the process takes place at a very intense rate, and then slows down for a while. The society then assimilates the changes. Thus three major pulses of fragmentation have occurred in Russian history.

The first of these occurred in the second half of the sixteenth century, when literacy began to increase. After the Napoleonic Wars (and, more directly, the introduction of railroads), fragmentation intensified during the second and third quarters of the nineteenth centuries. And as a result of the simultaneous increase in literacy and electricity, fragmentation in Russia reached an intensity without precedent in world history in the second quarter of the twentieth century. Thus it happened in the Soviet period that there arose the interrelated commitments to a reference theory of meaning in language, representational painting, and the realist novel which literacy had produced in England and France in the nineteenth century. Because of the strong residual orality in Russia, it took the power of electricity to create these structures. Electricity thus generally had for Russians an opposite effect from that which it had in the relatively more literate parts of Europe.

The life and work of Lenin offer numerous examples of this extreme tension between orality and literacy in Russia. His writing style expresses this tension in predictable ways, for Lenin uses writing as oral polemic, which—as Ong and various anthropologists have shown —occurs as an institutionalized form of social interchange among oral peoples. Like a good polemicist, Lenin mocks his opponents and waxes ironic about their foibles. Since he is writing, not speaking, he often quotes long passages from people with whom he disagrees, so as to create the best semblance of dialogue the printed page allows. He strains to overcome the uniformity of print by frequent use of exclamation marks and italics. Yet one also notices the juxtaposition of folk proverbs with abstruse terminology. These literate terms suggest his paradoxical use of polemic as a monistic form—to deny interchange, and to annihilate his opponents. In the works of Lenin, and in the Soviet Union in general, polemic loses its binary nature and becomes an expression of the center's desire to destroy the margin. During the purges of the thirties, *Pravda* ran headlines such as "Kill the Snakes!"

Lenin's major theoretical work, *Materialism and Empiriocriticism* (1908), shows clearly the tension between the need for dichotomies and the need to deny the existence of dichotomies. He says, for example, "Recognizing the existence of objective reality, i.e., of matter in motion, independently of our consciousness, materialism must inevitably also recognize the objective reality of time and space."[24] In passionately affirming the assumptions of Newtonian physics three years after Einstein had proved those assumptions invalid, Lenin committed himself to the dichotomy objective–subjective, which in turn generates numerous other dichotomies such as materialist–idealist, progressive–reactionary, leftist–rightist, and so on. The commitment to these dichotomies also means that one must define epistemological problems out of existence, as Lenin does: "There is absolutely no difference in principle between the phenomenon and the thing in itself, and there cannot be any."[25] Although he is using Kant's terminology, he is denying Kant's dichotomy of phenomenon and neumenon by saying that one can achieve absolute knowledge. (This form of argument, like much else in Soviet thought, may simply express the tendency of the newly literate to create dichotomies while insisting that they are binary pairs.)

For Lenin, absolute knowledge comes to us through the eyes. He refers approvingly to Engels on this point: "Engels speaks neither of symbols nor of hieroglyphs [as images for knowledge], but of copies, photographs, representations, mirror reflections of things."[26] A belief in absolute knowledge thus means a reliance on sight as the primary cognitive sense. Since visual imagery has such prestige for newly literate people, Russians repeat over and over again that, for example, "Art reflects reality." As an enterprising Czech critic has shown, the official Soviet theory of aesthetics depends completely on this visual imagery.[27]

Visual imagery also occurs in a principle of Marxism that Stalin used in various ways, "The economic basis determines the ideological superstructure." This blatantly visual image expresses not merely a dichotomy, but a dichotomy whose prime function is to create a justification for isolating content from context. Stalin used this method of reasoning to demonstrate that assembly lines, for instance, in the Soviet Union have no similarity to assembly lines in the United States. Although assembly lines in the United States produce alienation and

24. V. I. Lenin, *Polnoe sobranie sochinenii,* 18:181.

25. Ibid., p. 102.

26. Ibid., pp. 244–45.

27. See Vladimir Karbusicky, *Wiederspiegelungstheorie und Strukturalismus.*

boredom, they do not—so goes the reasoning—have a similar effect in the Soviet Union, for the difference in economic bases produces different results from the same experience. This is abstraction of a high order, and only literates could think this way.

An enormous neon sign on the roof of the Moscow Hydroelectric Station reads: "Communism Is Soviet Power Plus Electrification of the Whole Country." This equation expresses very well Lenin's belief in electricity as a panacea. His first major statement on the subject dates from 1913, and sets the tone for all his subsequent ones:

> The "electrification" of all factories and railroads will make the condition of labor more hygienic, will rid millions of workers of smoke, dust, and dirt, will speed up the transformation of repulsive workshops into clean, light, laboratories worthy of man. Electrical light will rid millions of "domestic slaves" of the necessity of killing three quarters of their life in a foul-smelling kitchen.[28]

Lenin sounds as if he is writing promotional copy for General Electric. Quotations such as this show his reliance on electricity in the typical literate manner: solely as a means for improving living conditions.

Lenin assumed that the combination of Soviet power and electrification of the whole country would improve working conditions without altering their essential structure. He was right in that electricity intensified the centralization of power in the leader, a process that by 1917 had been going on for a thousand years in Russia.

The iconography of Lenin which one sees in art works everywhere in the Soviet Union expresses this recurrent center–margin relationship very well, for they almost invariably represent him with his arm outstretched, either gesticulating or leading the people onward. (Significantly, when Soviet paintings and statues show Lenin in repose, he is writing.) The motif of the outstretched arm in fact appears canonical in Soviet realism. Workers thrust forth their hammers, collective farmers their sickles, and guerrilla soldiers their rifles—all in a similar manner.

By expressing a relationship of center to margin, the motif of the outstretched arm denies the autonomy of the body, and by implication the autonomy of any structure at all, while at the same time it expresses the continuity of space. The motif appears soon after the rise of perspective in the Renaissance, when supplementary figures point

28. Lenin, *Polnoe sobranie sochinenii,* 23:94–95.

to the saint or hero, and appropriately continues in the work of the painter who best expressed Louis XIV's centralization of power, Charles Le Brun. The outstretched arm virtually becomes a cliché in romantic painting after David's *Bonaparte on Mount St. Bernard* (1800), and Delacroix's *Liberty Leading the People, 1830* (1830).

The continuity between romanticism and socialist realism as expressions of a newly literate sensibility appears clearly if one compares *Liberty Leading the People* with the world's tallest statue, the 270-foot *Motherland,* which stands just outside Volgograd. The enormous female figure leads the way to the future (spatialized as always in linear tribalism) just as the female figure in Delacroix does; she holds a sword in her outstretched right arm, and beckons to the masses with her left.

One can distinguish between the iconography of Lenin and that of Stalin by noticing the implications of the placement of their arms. Whereas Lenin gesticulates, writes, or in some way refers to the external world, Stalin never does. Like a Buddha, Stalin has a self-contained quality; he sometimes smokes a pipe, as Lenin never does in a portrait. In fact, one work by Aleksandr Gerasimov, *Stalin and Voroshilov at the Kremlin* (1938), shows the similarity of socialist realism to religious painting. In this work, which Gerasimov completed before the signing of the Nazi-Soviet nonaggression pact, Stalin and Voroshilov stand on the Kremlin wall in order to keep a watchful eye on the West, on Germany. The painting conforms to all the demands of representational art except one: Gerasimov depicts Stalin as taller than Voroshilov, whereas Voroshilov was in fact taller than Stalin. Gerasimov denies visual reality for the same reason that medieval painters depicted saints and kings as taller than the common folk; Stalin's importance, not his height, determined his iconographic image.

In the post-Stalin period, the most severe tensions of the conflict between orality and literacy have lessened, but the very structure of the society generates them, and they will not cease to have an effect. In the last quarter of the twentieth century they may increase again, as Russians who have experienced three generations of literacy and urban life have to deal with computers, television, and atomic energy.

Chapter 13

Tribal Linearity

In the United States, the most literate country in the history of the world, implosion has caused the rise, not of linear tribalism, but of tribal linearity. As we have seen, tribal linearity differs from linear tribalism in its lack of awareness of totality. For most of the twentieth century, it has never occurred to literate Americans that Einstein's theories, or modern art generally, could have any bearing on their lives, and people therefore have not denounced them, as various representatives of tribal linearity have done.

But when by chance modern art forced itself upon the consciousness of tribal linearity, its representatives have felt the threat it poses, and have attacked it exactly as Stalinists have. In *Art Under a Dictatorship,* Lehmann-Haupt cites the comments by Congressman Fred E. Busbey with regard to an exhibit "Advancing American Art," which the State Department sent abroad in 1947.

> The movement of modern art is a revolution against the conventional and natural things of life as expressed in art. . . . The artists of the radical school ridicule all that has been held dear in art. . . . Without exception, the paintings in the State Department group that portray a person make him or her unnatural. The skin is not reproduced as it would be naturally, but as sullen ashen gray. Features of the face are always depressed and melancholy. . . . That is what the Communists and other extremists want to portray. They want to tell foreigners that the American people are despondent, broken down, or of hideous shape—thoroughly dissatisfied with their lot, and eager for a change of government.[1]

The United States has also staged its own purge trials of degenerate art. Jules Langsner gave the following account of one that occurred in Los Angeles in 1951.

1. Quoted in Helmut Lehmann-Haupt, *Art Under a Dictatorship,* pp. 239–40.

For six weeks artists of Los Angeles have shuddered in a common nightmare. Reality, bordering on the grotesque, descended on them all when our city council put "on trial" a group of works removed from the walls of the City's Greek Theater Annual Exhibition, and brought them into City Hall, there to be held up to scorn and ridicule. Like a great tornado, the City Councilmen grabbed at large for victims. . . .

It was hard to believe that it was really happening. Hundreds of respected, sober citizens present at the hearing heard a Sanity-in-Art witness testify that "Modern Art" is actually a means of espionage, and that if you know how to read them, modern paintings will disclose the weak spots in U.S. fortifications and such crucial constructions as Boulder Dam.[2]

These two quotations show that in tribal linearity, as in linear tribalism, art has a cognitive value.

A casual reference by William L. Shirer may serve to begin a discussion of the sociopolitical similarities between linear tribalism and tribal linearity.

The Reich Youth Leader was Baldur von Schirach, a romantically minded young man and an energetic organizer, whose mother was an American and whose great-grandfather, a Union officer, had lost a leg at Bull Run; he told his American jailers at Nuremberg that he had become an anti-Semite at the age of seventeen after reading a book called *Eternal Jew,* by Henry Ford.[3]

In the United States, the financial empires that were a result of the railroads caused intense centralization. The apologists for financial centralization then evolved the highly literate, deterministic ideas of social Darwinism. In turn, social Darwinism appeared as racial determinism in Germany and economic (often mixed with racial) determinism in Russia.

That the primary institution of tribal linearity in the United States, the corporation, depends historically on the hybrid nature of the automobile emerges clearly from the history of the medium. Ford built his Model T in the image of literacy, as he in effect acknowledged in his famous slogan, "A customer can have a car painted any color he

2. Quoted in ibid., p. 241.
3. Shirer, *The Rise and Fall of the Third Reich,* p. 149.

wants so long as it is black." The customer had no possibility of personal involvement or choice in selecting the machine, each of which was like every other one. But the hand crank made starting the Model T so difficult and dangerous that the real development had to await the advent of electricity in 1911: "The electric starter was soon acclaimed as a major invention, for it made the automobile, at least potentially, a universal vehicle."[4]

Only an electrical device could have made operating and driving an automobile safe enough, and easy enough, to attract a mass market. As we know, it made the automobile a hybrid medium. Once Charles Franklin Kettering, the inventor of the electric starter, had demonstrated its efficiency, the assembly line rapidly followed. Unless one believes in the Marxist dichotomy basis–superstructure, the assembly line (Ford's began on 14 January 1914),[5] whether it operated in the United States, Germany, or Russia, meant ever greater speedup. Those in power exhorted the workers to ever greater production, which meant ever greater fragmentation.

Ford's career corresponds to the two-stage evolution of tribal linearity. When he began manufacturing the Model T, Ford appeared as the champion of the common people against the wealthy, who had bought the first automobiles during the 1890s as ostentatious luxuries. (The Volkswagen had a similar social and class significance when it first appeared.) Ford also appeared as the champion of his own workers. Nine days before the assembly line began operations, the Ford management announced the "Five-Dollar Day." A social historian summarized the principle features of the plan in the following way:

> To give concrete effect to its [Ford management's] humanitarian motives, it was instituting a basic "Five-Dollar Day," thus doubling the prevailing wage-scale for common labor. Furthermore, it was reducing the working day from nine hours to eight. The whole plan was based upon the principle of sharing anticipated profits; those for 1914 were estimated as being sufficient to justify a distribution among the workers of some ten million dollars. From the benefits of the plan, no "qualified employee" was to be excluded, not even "the lowliest laborer and the man who merely sweeps the floors."[6]

4. Lloyd Morris, *Not So Long Ago,* p. 321.
5. Ibid., p. 338.
6. Ibid., p. 342.

At the time, Ford

> . . . seemed . . . to be as inspired a reformer as Miss [Jane]
> Adams herself, as deeply imbued with the principles expressed
> by Hull House and other social settlements. For he set up a
> "Sociological Department," the private equivalent of a public
> welfare agency, to minister to the needs of his workers, many of
> whom were foreign-born and recent immigrants.[7]

Dr. Samuel Marquis resigned the deanship of St. Paul's Cathedral in
Detroit to administer this department, and thereby became a symbolic
figure.

Marquis represents the tribal element of a tribal linearity, and
when centralization began, he suffered a far milder version of the fate
of all the tribal elements in linear tribalism in Eastern Europe.

> Dr. Marquis, who began his mission with practically unlimited
> means at his disposal, and certainly with boundless hope,
> resigned after five years, a deeply disillusioned man. And Henry
> Ford then explained to the world that welfare was out of date.[8]

Ford justified his own centralization of power by saying, "Business
holds no place for democracy . . . if by democracy is meant the
shaping of policies by the vote of a large number of people or their
delegates."[9] And, to enforce centralization, Ford appointed one Harry
Herbert Bennet as head of the "Service Department," which he used
as "a private militia, proficient in the arts of espionage, terrorism and
labor-baiting."[10] Moreover, Bennet's men resembled the members of
the SS and NKVD, who had similar functions: "[They were] the most
brutal, vicious and conscienceless thugs . . . who could be counted
upon to accept an opportunity to indulge their sadistic desires in lieu
of additional compensation."[11] Finally, "An Englishwoman touring
the country [Russia] in 1926 reported that she saw Ford's name em-
blazoned on banners in workers' processions, as emblematic of a new
era."[12]

These external similarities between the careers of Ford and Stalin

7. Ibid., p. 344.
8. Ibid., p. 353.
9. Ibid., p. 358.
10. Ibid., p. 361.
11. Ibid., p. 367.
12. Reported in Allan Nevins and Frank Ernest Hill, *Ford. II: Expansion
and Challenge,* p. 673.

suggest that structural similarities existed between their psyches as well; by relating the two men, it becomes possible to resolve the dichotomy between the individual and the social process that many books on history describe.

Let us begin the analysis with an obvious fact, that both men exhibited considerable aggression toward the world. The differing results of this aggression, which were relatively limited in Ford's case, and unprecedented and unequaled in Stalin's case, show us again how fragmentation has saved the United States from violence, and how the lack of fragmentation in Russia created the potential for mass slaughter. When Ford disliked a man, he had him fired; when Stalin disliked a man, he had him shot. Likewise, Ford merely *said,* "History is bunk." Stalin *acted* on that assumption and did his best to destroy history. The multiplicity of power centers in America made it impossible for Ford to control the country (more on this later, with regard to Richard Nixon); once Stalin gained control of the Central Committee, he had the power of life and death over everyone in the country. Thus, numbers of people killed have little relevance if one wants to elicit structural similarities.

To do so, one can generalize the terminology of Thomas A. Harris's *I'm OK—You're OK* to apply it to social, as well as psychological, processes. As most people know by now, Harris defines mature adults as those who can manifest behavior that implies both self-respect, and respect for others. Their dialogue with the world thus says, "I'm OK—You're OK." Few people achieve such integration, of course; we more commonly encounter either the dichotomy "I'm OK —You're not OK," or "I'm not OK—You're OK." (Harris reserves the extreme of "I'm not OK—You're not OK" primarily for autistic children.) It is the first formulation that interests us here, because it characterizes both the center-margin structure and the individual psyches as well of Ford and Stalin.

Stalin's refusal to admit mistakes and his obsessive need for purges require no documentation here, of course. As for Ford, Anne Jardim, in her brilliant book, *The First Henry Ford: A Study in Personality and Business Leadership,* makes the following statement:

> Linking all the stages of Ford's need for control—from the administration of the company to the manufacture of the car, to Ford's belief in his own infallibility and the wider horizons this opened to him—there is a single dominant theme. This is the

need to act in the face of an external threat, the need for
absolute control in order to ward off and where possible
destroy the threat which existed somewhere "out there."[13]

For Ford and Stalin, all those "out there" were not OK; they couldn't
be. If some people were OK, that fact would mean that the self was
not OK, for such people can think only in dichotomies. And the more
they struggled to maintain this dichotomy between the self and others,
the more violence they created.

Harris makes an intriguing guess about the genesis of the structure
"I'm OK—You're not OK." In the following passage, he uses to term
self-stroking to refer to the way children can bestow their own self-
respect:

> I believe this self-stroking does in fact occur during the time a
> little person is healing from major painful injuries such as are
> inflicted on a youngster who has come to be known as "the
> battered child." . . . I believe that it is while this little individual
> is healing . . . that he experiences a sense of comfort alone and
> by himself, if for no other reason than that his improvement is
> in such contrast to the gross pain he has just experienced. It is
> as if he senses, I'll be all right if you leave me alone. I'm OK by
> myself. As the brutal parents reappear, he may shrink in horror
> that it will happen again. You hurt me! You are not OK. I'm OK
> —You're not OK. The early history of many criminal psycho-
> paths, who occupy this position, reveal this kind of gross
> physical abuse.[14]

Stalin conforms very well to this pattern, for one of the few generally
known facts about his childhood is that his father beat him repeatedly.
Ford's sense of "not OK" also derives from his father, but in a more
subtle fashion. Jardim develops a most persuasive argument (which I
cannot cite in full here) that Ford's narcissism, rigidity, and fear of
innovation expressed an unresolved Oedipal complex, and thus involved aggression displaced from his idealized mother onto his father.
Jardim shows, for example, that Ford distorted the facts at will in order
to create for himself the myth of a harsh, unjust father. However, if
we examine the development of these psychic tensions, rather than
their genesis, we again find analogies.

13. Anne Jardim, *The First Henry Ford: A Study in Personality and Business Leadership* (Cambridge: The MIT Press, 1970), p. 76.
14. Thomas A. Harris, *I'm OK—You're OK,* pp. 48–49.

Jardim assumes that Ford's obsessive need to build a car for the farmer, and his refusal to allow innovations (even when bankruptcy threatened the company as a result of the competition from Chevrolet in the twenties) came from his guilt about his relationship with his father. Moreover, the fabulous success of the Ford plant at Highland Park seemed to justify this whole attitude; it justified his belief that he was acting rationally. Likewise, the revolution probably confirmed Stalin's attitude that as a revolutionary he was OK, but that the czarist regime was clearly not OK.

Given this seeming confirmation of the "I'm OK—You're not OK" structure, Ford and Stalin then moved to obtain absolute control over their enterprises, and were successful. As we know, Stalin—like Hitler in Germany—refused to allow any coherent bureaucratic structure to exist in Russia. While we expect this fear of memos and organizational charts in oral societies, we certainly do not expect it in one of the largest corporations in America. But as long as Henry Ford remained president of Ford Motor Company, it merely expressed the state of his psyche at the given moment. And Ford retained many of the oral qualities of his Irish grandfather; he believed that one learned through touch, not sight, and he never was able to read blueprints. Hence, he once boasted, "The Ford factories and enterprises have no organization, no specific duties attaching to any position, no line of succession or of authority, very few titles, and no conferences."[15] Mutatis mutandis, he might have been describing the Central Committee of the Communist Party. Since Ford could not allow the existence of a bureaucratic structure that might resist a display of aggression, the predictable chaos so familiar to us from the comments of people who knew Hitler and Stalin resulted.

Speaking of aggression, it is important to understand that the choice of those identified as "not OK" is a random one. Ford, like Stalin, was probably not anti-Semitic in any real sense—the career of the *Dearborn Independent* and the "doctors' plot" notwithstanding. Both men needed enemies whom they would label "not OK," and the tribal identity of the Jews made them easy targets. Since both men thought in dichotomies, they very easily absolved themselves of any guilt for the violence of their aggression by creating the dichotomy power–responsibility. Although they had total control, violence was always someone else's fault.

15. Quoted in Jardim, p. 114.

As we know, Ford's career has the bipartite structure that characterizes the development of totalitarian regimes in the twentieth century; a purge divides the two parts. Hence, at this point, I would like to follow Earle Stanley Gardner's device in his Ellery Queen mysteries and pose a challenge to the reader: Does the following quotation apply to the Russian government under Stalin, or to the Ford Motor Company under Henry Ford?

> There was a great deal of apprehension, because every day, purges were going on. Departments were being eliminated overnight. These purges were not conducted on a scientific basis. Departments were completely wiped out.[16]

The stiffness of the phrasing, and the pseudoscientific terminology suggest a Russian origin for this statement, but in fact it comes from someone who witnessed Ford's purges of major executives in 1920–1921.

There are, then, numerous similarities between American corporations such as Ford Motor Company and General Electric, and the Communist Party of the Soviet Union. However much the content of the thought patterns of the top five hundred executives in the United States may differ from those of the top five hundred members of the Communist Party, the structure generally coincides. These men have similar social origins, dress alike, pursue their careers in a hierarchy that has similar rules, and they have similar attitudes about the society their decisions affect. Like General Electric, the Communist Party considers progress its most important product. General Electric has greatly increased the literacy (in both the direct and the indirect sense) of Americans, and the Communist Party has done the same for Russians.

In Part I of this book, I distinguished between the two subsets, or halves of a dichotomy, that constitute the linear paradigm: the continuous subset, which emphasizes the continuity of the line, and the noncontinuous subset, which emphasizes the axiom that a line consists of an infinite number of points. We will gain a great deal for the understanding of the history of the United States and the Soviet Union in the twentieth century if we contrast the two countries by associating literacy in the United States with the noncontinuous subset of the linear paradigm, and literacy in the Soviet Union with the continuous

16. Ibid., p. 121.

subset. In the United States, the noncontinuous subset of the linear paradigm means a commitment to attitudes such as individualism, concern with physical satisfaction and appearance; in the Soviet Union, the other half of the dichotomy emphasizes fulfillment through carrying out the centralization of power—and ultimately, the centralization of knowledge and meaning.

In the twentieth century, the two countries have tended to look at each other from opposite halves of the same dichotomy. Each has difficulty in admitting the existence of the other half of the dichotomy —and hence a similarity—within itself. The tension of suppressing this aspect of itself creates a need to overemphasize the importance of movements within the other country that threaten that country: Just as Angela Davis represents the United States to Russians in a way that millions of American citizens would find repugnant, Aleksandr Solzhenitsyn represents Russia to Americans in a way that millions of Russians would find repugnant.

For analogous reasons, each country finds the popular arts in the other country perplexing. Americans find Russian popular culture naive and propagandistic, while Russians find American popular culture self-indulgent and pornographic. Historically, both countries have had difficulty in distinguishing between the noncontinuous subset of the linear paradigm and the nonlinear paradigm. Literate people in both countries tend to label them simply as "decadent." The fear of decadence expresses a similar need in both countries, a need to preserve the dichotomy between past and present in the form of cultural and intellectual innocence. Innocence presumably brings happiness, and thus we understand the relationship between innocence and the obligatory happy ending of American and Soviet popular art. Robert Warshow has this to say on the subject:

> Modern equalitarian societies, . . . whether democratic or authoritarian in their political forms, always base themselves on the claim that they are making life happier; the avowed function of the modern state, at least in its ultimate terms, is not only to regulate social relations, but also to determine the quality and possibilities of human life in general. Happiness thus becomes the chief political issue—in a sense, the only political issue—and for that reason it can never be treated as an issue at all. If an American or a Russian is unhappy, it implies a certain reprobation of his society, and therefore . . . it becomes an obligation of citizenship to be cheerful; if the authorities find it

necessary, the citizen may even be compelled to make a public display of his cheerfulness on important occasions.[17]

Warshow concludes this analysis with the telling comment, "Every production of mass culture is a public act and must conform with accepted notions of the public good."[18] We realize, too, that the happy ending expresses not only "accepted notions of the public good," but also accepted notions of space. Happiness needs continuous space in order to flow from the center to the margin, and this continuous space creates the determinism of the belief that "Crime never pays," and "Justice always triumphs."

A recent copy of *Pravda* illustrated the operation of the continuous subset of the linear paradigm in the Soviet Union very well when it printed on the front page a letter from one Leida Peips, a milkmaid on a collective farm in Estonia, to Leonid Brezhnev. Peips's letter begins:

> Dear Leonid Ilyich! I want to share a great joy with you. Today my cherished dream was realized: I became a candidate member of the multi-million party of Lenin.
>
> The Call of the Central Committee of the Communist Party of the Soviet Union has filled this year with particular content. To live every hour of labor, every work day with the thought of personal responsibility for the affairs of the country—this is precisely how the workers of my native collective farm will answer this Call.[19]

Americans will probably respond to this letter with a condescending smile. If asked why, they would probably mention what they perceive as Peips's naiveté and her hyperbolic style. In structural terms, such people may well be feeling their own separateness from the state threatened by the meaning that flows from the state into Leida Peips's life. A Russian would respond in a similar way if an American showed him a corresponding document, a letter from a housewife endorsing a product in an advertisement, for the housewife would speak of the happiness that the corporation's product had given her and her family. The American who identifies himself as a Budweiser drinker and a

17. Robert Warshow, "The Gangster as Tragic Hero," in *The Immediate Experience,* pp. 127–28.
18. Ibid., p. 451.
19. *Pravda,* 5 February 1975, p. 1.

Ford owner thus has a counterpart in the Soviet Union who identifies himself as a Party member or a worker who overfulfills his norm.

The general use of the newspaper medium in the two countries differs in a similar way. Newspapers in the two countries offer a roughly comparable amount of hard information (although American newspapers do more of this than Russian newspapers). They differ in that American newspapers offer primarily "points of view"—sometimes about news and politics, to be sure, but more often about personal life ("Dear Abby," for example), cooking, household hints, and so forth. No point of view, or report of a debate about policy, can appear in *Pravda,* of course, for Russians use print to express its original effect, the centralization of power. *Pravda* has no point of view, and any article (or even any poem) that seems to state one, actually expresses the Party's position on a given issue at a given time. Hence, *Pravda* carries no "human interest" stories (reports of floods or airplane crashes, for example), while newspaper editorials in the United States lack the authority of editorials in *Pravda.*

A relationship seems to obtain between the emphasis on discrete detail—what is impressionistically called individualism—and visual appeal, which invites the eye to focus on specifics without moving on to the larger whole. Thus the United States produces the shiny, gleaming products that most people associate with capitalism, packages them in bright colors, and displays them in shiny, gleaming stores. By contrast, Russians suppress visual appeal (with the significant exceptions of rockets and airplanes) and manufacture very crude cosmetics and clothing. In the absence of General Electric and Westinghouse, the electrification of the Russian kitchen of which Lenin dreamed in 1913 has not taken place, except in the apartments and dachas of the party elite, who buy their appliances in West Germany.

This ambivalence toward literacy involves more than high-definition surfaces. In the twenties, for example, the Soviets expressed their desire to fragment society as quickly as possible by replacing icons with printed signs—a phenomenon that the many satirists of the time mocked with great success. Yet the oral Russians could not manufacture something as necessary in a literary society as a pencil, and the astute American capitalist Armand Hammer made a fortune by importing Eberhard Faber's pencils and selling them in the Soviet Union. (Similarly, Americans found that ballpoint pens made very desirable gifts for Russians in the sixties.) This same ambivalence appears in the organization of Soviet cities, where the fragmentation of a total area into a telephone book is unthinkable. If you want the telephone number of a specific person, you ask for it at a kiosk. (You must know the person's full name, address, *and* date of birth.) Moscow looks like a city, but functions like a village in which rumors of, say, a shipment of oranges in January can cause a near riot.

The Russians' reluctance to commit themselves wholeheartedly to fragmentation has affected their governmental structure, for they have never allowed written laws to have any real authority. Even today, the Central Committee of the Communist Party of the Soviet Union has no rules, no distribution of responsibilities, and—above all —no terms of office. Such an unstable situation may well correspond to a deep need of the people, for throughout Russian history, the Russians' have avoided government service because of their fear of literacy. And as a result, they have tended to allow those who have confronted the frightening experience of literacy in government to do anything they have wanted.

Since one half of a dichotomy never becomes completely dissociated from the other half, people who insist on the exclusive significance of one half of a dichotomy in their lives consequently have little capacity to understand or control the other half when it appears. Capitalists who assert their belief in free enterprise exert great effort to establish monopolies, and Communists who assert their belief in democracy create elitist governments. Thus, the history of both the Soviet Union and the United States shows the importance of the other half of the dichotomy as well—the one which the country in question does not like to recognize.

In a way that recalls Marinetti's evolution from art to totalitarian politics, the theme of Prometheanism, of extreme individual assertion, characterized much of the symbolist era in Russian prerevolutionary culture, and it continued after the revolution as well. For example, people usually think of the thirties in the Soviet Union as a period of great oppression and deprivation of civil liberties. But to assume that this was all that happened is to forget the people who carried out fragmentation—the members of the secret police and the party hierarchy. For these people, the thirties and the forties constituted a period of nearly complete individualism. Solzhenitsyn makes us aware of this when he addresses one of the "blue hats," or members of the secret police, in *The Gulag Archipelago:*

Any object you've seen is yours! Any apartment you've found is yours! Any woman is yours! Any enemy disappears! The earth under your foot is yours! The sky is yours, it's blue!![20]

Many people in this period lived a life of ease and comfort. They often acquired considerable personal wealth, particularly after World War II, when the Russians raided and confiscated art treasures and other valuables from those parts of Europe they had occupied. The relative size of this elite group was probably as significant as that of the French nobility in the eighteenth century.

The Russian establishment understands very well something that McLuhan said about cameras:

"Conspicuous consumption" owed less to the phrase of Veblen than to the press photographer, who began to invade the entertainment spots of the very rich. The sights of men ordering drinks from horseback at the bars of clubs quickly caused a public revulsion that drove the rich into the ways of timid mediocrity and obscurity in America, which they have never abandoned. The photograph made it quite unsafe to come out and play, for it betrayed such blatant dimensions of power as to be self-defeating. (pp. 200–201)

This analysis, in its negative aspect, applies equally well to the media situation in the Soviet Union. Thus references to the private lives of the privileged party members, scientists, and writers never appear in the press, nor do references to their elaborate systems of secret shops, restaurants, and clubs.

In the United States, the continuous subset of the linear paradigm that has generally predominated in Russia has appeared not only in the corporation but also in politics, in the centralization of power in the presidency. Radio speeded up this process, of course, but not as destructively as it did in Germany. Liberals, as the prime representatives of literacy in American politics, welcomed this change, for it meant a weakening of such essential tribal concepts as local autonomy. With television, this process reached a breaking point, which itself lasted some six years, from the summer of 1968 to the summer of 1974.

Television involved people more directly than ever before in the mechanics of the centralization of power, when they saw the violence of the police riots that took place during the Democratic party's con-

20. Aleksandr Solzhenitsyn, *Arkhipelag Gulag,* p. 160.

vention in 1968. As a result, the words *liberal* and *conservative* exchanged meanings. After August of 1968, liberals generally opposed the centralization of power that the Civil Rights Act, for example, had institutionalized, and conservatives defended it. The millions of people who felt threatened by implosion, as Carnap's physicist had in 1930, elected Richard Nixon, during whose presidency the breaking point finally occurred.

Nixon's presidency shows many of the same features as administrations of other heads of state who also had linear thought patterns. His recurrent musings on his place in history, for instance, represent a particularly American version of Louis XIV's *gloire*. More specifically, though, his presidency shows how the institutionalized fragmentation of American society prevented centralization from becoming as complete as it did in the vastly simpler Russian situation. Like Stalin, Nixon isolated himself from the working mechanisms of government, and his chief aide, H. R. Haldeman, controlled both access to the leader, and what the leader knew. A Georgian, Aleksandr Poskrybyshev, had a comparable function under Stalin and wielded comparable power. To complete the analogy, both Haldeman and Poskrybyshev were completely sincere and unselfish in their devotion to centralization.

Since Nixon could not destroy other power centers as readily as Stalin could, there arose the constant tension with the government bureaucracy and with the press which characterized the Nixon years. These two frustrated institutions combined to publish the facts about the Watergate break-in, which led to Nixon's resignation in the summer of 1974. Incidentally, during the previous summer, television made people aware of the highly literate thought patterns of the Nixon administration. Erlichman, Mitchell, and the others used the spatialized imagery of the phrase "at that point in time" so frequently that it became permanently associated with them. As the publication of the transcription of the White House tapes showed, Nixon himself could not think without using spatialized imagery, and the dichotomies that imagery implies.[21]

As a highly literate person, and hence a believer in content, Nixon could not understand the difference between a document, which centralizes power, and a tape recording, which decentralizes it. Natu-

21. For a computer-assisted study of Nixon's spatialized imagery, see Geoffrey Miller, "The Story of P."

rally, then, he had no awareness of the magical appeal of the tapes which he had made. The attraction exerted by the possibility of actually hearing his deliberations with his subordinates proved so great that Nixon himself could not withstand it. The devices that he thought would immortalize his centralization of power, thus in fact ended it, in a classical example of the reversal of an overheated medium.

Nixon's resignation did not end the similarities to Stalin's tenure in office, but perpetuated these similarities in the reaction of the two governments to the problem of the past. Literate governments make the relationship of the past to the present a dichotomy, and hence we may never know the full extent of the crimes which people committed during the Nixon and Stalin years. The American government's inability to punish criminals who acted in the name of the centralization of power corresponds to the inability of the Soviet government to deal with those who committed analogous, if more extreme, crimes during the Stalin era. But a thorough analysis cannot stop here; it must emphasize the fact that this dichotomy of past–present exists in the general public in both countries as well. Literate societies find it difficult to separate the historical individual from the symbolic office that he holds into a binary pair, and hence millions of Americans and Russians will go to their graves believing in the essential innocence of Nixon and Stalin. Such people conceive of the individual as a visual image of national identity. Distinguishing between the two would cause too much psychic pain. Their desires thus correspond to those of the government.

Ultimately, Stalin died and Nixon resigned. The processes they represent continue, of course, but processes evolve.[22] The second pulse of electrification in the United States began after World War II with the emergence of television as a mass medium. Television, a cooler medium than film (the tension between the two makes the aesthetic structure of the film *The Last Picture Show*), began to cool off American popular culture in the fifties.

22. Much in this analysis also applies to European countries that have residual orality such as Spain, Portugal, and Ireland, as well as to the manifestations of linear tribalism that have appeared in South America and Africa during the sixties and seventies. The use of electricity in torture in these countries serves as yet another reminder of the medium's capacity to fragment.

Chapter 14

Rock 'n' Roll and Rock—
And Now What?

We come after.
—George Steiner

George Steiner[1] means, "We come after totalitarianism and must somehow learn to live with that fact." We also come after modernism and must somehow learn to live with that fact as well. For the contemporary theorist, working with the relationship between modernism and postmodernism offers a most stimulating challenge, as Leslie Fiedler suggests:

Almost all living readers and writers are aware of a fact which they have no adequate words to express, not in English certainly, not even in American. We are living, have been living for two decades—and have become acutely conscious of the fact since 1955—through the death throes of Modernism and the birth pangs of Post-Modernism. The kind of literature which had arrogated to itself the name Modern (with the presumption that it represented the ultimate advance in sensibility and form, that beyond it newness was not possible), and whose moment of triumph lasted from a point just before World War I until one just after World War II, is *dead,* i.e., belongs to history not actuality. In the field of the novel, this means that the age of Proust, Mann, and Joyce is over: just as in verse that of T.S. Eliot, Paul Valéry, Montale and Seferis is done with. Obviously, *this* fact has not remained secret: and some critics have, indeed, been attempting to deal with its implications. But they have been trying to do it in a language and with methods which are singularly inappropriate, since both method and language were invented by the defunct Modernists themselves to apologize for their own work and the work of their preferred literary ancestors (John Donne, for instance, or the *symbolistes*), and to educate an audience

1. George Steiner, *Language and Silence,* p. ix.

capable of responding to them. Naturally, this will not do at all.[2]

The general acceptance of modernist art has resulted in its taking on the stature of a kind of classicism; the rebels have become the academy. Art that no longer threatens may retain its beauty, but it belongs to the past: we must understand it in order to incorporate the past, yet we can understand the present only by responding to the images and experiences of the present.

While postmodernism has a definite continuity with modernism, it differs from it in at least three ways: 1) the substitution of process for the modernist opposition of space and time; 2) a conscious emphasis on binarism; and 3) the formative experience of popular culture. This last chapter will draw on all three of these characteristics, but especially the last one, in analyzing the music that created the postmodernist sensibility in the fifties and sixties.

Although both McLuhan (in *Understanding Media*) and Ong (in *Romance, Rhetoric, and Technology*) have done some work with popular music, I want to write about it here not because they have, but because doing so means merging my personal and professional motivations. Elvis Presley and the Beatles have meant a lot to me; moreover, their lingering presence in my consciousness had made me unable to use paradigms that make a dichotomy between popular and high culture.

This book has emphasized the holistic nature of the nonlinear paradigm in general and of McLuhan's work in particular; I want to conclude it with the discussion of rock 'n' roll because I believe that any contemporary paradigm that makes holistic claims must have the capacity to deal seriously and, above all, without condescension with popular culture as an aspect of social process. If, as McLuhan believes, media structure historical processes, then they structure all aspects of those processes and thus popular culture. If the analyst who works with a holistic paradigm disdains popular culture, then he or she simply has not internalized the paradigm.[3] While dichotomies do

2. Leslie Fiedler, "Cross the Border, Close the Gap," in *The Collected Essays of Leslie Fiedler,* pp. 461–62. Fiedler's emphasis.

3. I consider it a serious shortcoming of French structuralism that it has not generally dealt with popular culture. The lack of interest in popular culture on the part of French critics contrasts strikingly with the attitudes of French artists. One thinks, for instance, of the distinctly pop sensibility which Michel Butor expresses in *Mobile* as well as in other works. French critics no doubt neglect popular culture for analogous reasons to those which make them

remain in postmodernism, the serious analyst can and will minimize them.

One can use a genuinely rich nonlinear paradigm on a great variety of materials. The paradigm is, ideally, indifferent to the material on which one uses it. Therefore, I wish to show here that since modernism and postmodernism both came into existence as manifestations of implosion, the sociological patterns and recurring motifs that I found in the modernist material of the preceding chapter have analogues in postmodernist phenomena. In addition to demonstrating further the power of the paradigm, these analyses will suggest the pervasive continuity between modernism and postmodernism.

In working with popular culture, an emphasis on the concept of function has a great advantage because it tends to preclude, or at least make difficult, value judgments of the kind which reject popular culture as undignified, or unworthy of serious inquiry. To take a simplistic example, a car must have both pistons and wheels. It makes no sense to prefer pistons to wheels, or wheels to pistons; they simply have different functions. To apply the concept of function in comparing historical processes, however, one must work in a more abstract way; one must compare, not specific phenomena, but the similar function of different phenomena in the respective periods. One therefore asks, not "Is this good or bad?" but "What role in the given historical process did phenomenon X have?"

Thus, if we notice that Picasso's painting sometimes refers to African masks, and Roy Lichtenstein's painting to comics, we may conclude that primitivism functioned for modernism as popular culture functions for postmodernism. (Similarly, one could compare the role of folk music in the work of Bartók and Stravinsky to the role of blues music in the development of rock 'n' roll.) The cool structures of primitivism and popular culture have offered artists a vocabulary with which they could express implosion, and they have offered theorists ample justification for their principles—Worringer used primitivism as McLuhan used popular culture. The analogy also calls our attention to the fact that any period of implosion can only resolve dichotomies gradually, and never all at once. Thus, primitivism and popular culture in their respective periods have both had the effect of

---

neglect technology. Their implicit assumptions about what a Parisian intellectual should, and should not, do demonstrate the inertial force of French nationalism in an international age. See my "Marshall McLuhan and French Structuralism."

resolving the dichotomy high culture–low culture.

The period and general aesthetics of modernism, art nouveau, and cubism correspond roughly to the two postmodernist periods of popular music, rock 'n' roll (which lasted from 1955 to 1964), and rock (which lasted from 1964 to 1970). Artists who had grown up, respectively, with art nouveau and rock 'n' roll used these styles in their early work, and then destroyed them by creating cubism and rock. When Bob Dylan began playing the electric guitar, it marked the changeover from rock 'n' roll to rock and shocked many of his fans, just as Picasso shocked Matisse and even Braque when he painted *Les Demoiselles d'Avignon.*

Media complexes structured these four interrelated processes in various ways. If art nouveau expressed the age of the telephone, and cubism the age of the radio, rock 'n' roll expressed the natural association of two hybrid media, the automobile and the AM radio. In turn, stereophonic sound—a binary experience—gave rise to rock, and long-playing albums and FM radio became the creative media. Each period perceived the previous one as literate in various ways, and at the beginning of each new period, the major artists of the previous one suffered a certain disorientation.

But at this point something McLuhan's critics liked to notice becomes relevant; McLuhan *wrote* about orality; he used print to discuss demise of print (or so it seemed in the sixties). I find myself expressing a similar contradiction in that I am using the print of a university press to discuss music, and worse yet—popular music. "Worse yet," because popular music expresses the contradiction of our age in a greatly amplified way. On one hand, popular music has structured the perception and consciousness of many of us; we have shared it, and it has thus become a paradigm. On the other hand, and a powerful hand it is, popular music comes from big business, and thus conforms to the structure of other types of Big Business In America. Although the musicians themselves have little to do with literacy, their lawyers and record companies emphatically have a great deal to do with literacy.

This situation affects our lives only if we wish to *write* about the music, and reproduce the words in print; I attempted to do so, and rapidly found out that musical revolutionaries (or their lawyers at least) still consider the songs private property and want to make as much money from them as they can. Thus, the nominal subject of this chapter, the tension between orality and literacy in popular music, structures it as well; I have used the quotes for which I could get permission and have simply referred to some of the songs that have meant the most to me, and to America.

Specific analysis may begin by noticing the striking similarity in the sociology of postmodernism and that of modernism. Just as most modernists came from areas of residual orality, virtually all the musicians who created rock 'n' roll came from the most oral part of the United States, the South. Elvis Presley was born in Mississippi, and Jerry Lee Lewis in Tennessee. Possibly even more significant are the Southern blacks: Fats Domino (Louisiana), Little Richard and Ray Charles (Georgia), and Chuck Berry (who moved to Missouri at an early age). These Southerners shared a good deal, not only early poverty, but also the extremely important tradition of communal singing in small Southern churches.

Elvis began singing in church, and recorded several albums of hymns. The very title of Ray Charles's hit of the fifties, "Hallelujah, I Just Love Her So" suggests a secular hymn. Virtually all black singers —Aretha Franklin, Dionne Warwicke, and even Chuck Berry—got their starts by singing in church, and those with ears attuned to the sound of gospel choirs can detect its echoes in their work. But here the paradox arises, for the very opportunities of mobility that television made possible meant fragmentation. Gospel singing in small Southern churches has a very tribal quality, and is certainly not art in the Renaissance sense. But "Hallelujah, I Just Love Her So" has turned gospel singing into art in just this sense. Thus the very fact that oral peoples can respond creatively to implosion means that they also experience fragmentation.

This dual process of fragmentation and implosion accounts for the disorientation and consequent violence—both physical and verbal —in the behavior of many blacks. (I am assuming, of course, that social oppression in all its forms occurs as a manifestation of fragmentation.) Among rock 'n' roll musicians, Little Richard shows this vacillation between religion and art most distinctly. When the engine of a plane on which he was flying (1961) caught fire, he made a vow to return to the ministry if he survived. He did survive and kept the vow, but began performing again in 1969.

The position of blacks thus resembles that of Jews in the earlier part of the twentieth century. In both cases, artistic success meant the renunciation of some integral aspects of the cultural heritage that made the success possible in the first place. Because fragmentation had begun earlier for Jews, we find them associated in American media history with radio (David Sarnoff and William Paley) and movies (Louis Mayer, Samuel Goldwyn, Adolph Zukor, and many others). However, with the important exceptions of Bob Dylan and Paul Simon, Jews did not have particular importance in rock 'n' roll, or in rock. Yet when we think of the way Irving Berlin, George and Ira Gershwin, Jerome Kern, and Richard Rodgers dominated American popular music in the first half of the twentieth century, Dylan and Simon seem isolated by comparison. What happened was that poor Southerners experienced fragmentation after World War II, as Jews had done after emigrating to America. This new music so speeded up the social process that it became general; I doubt that one can find significant patterns in the sociology of rock.

In the fifties, songs typically used the media which formed rock 'n' roll: a 45-rpm record over an AM radio in a car. Carl Belz, in *The Story of Rock,* discusses the changeover from the 78 rpm record to the 45 rpm record in very McLuhanesque terms.

> While its speed was slower, in all of its other features the 45 constituted a speeding-up process. This was true for everyone connected with the record: manufacturers, distributors, shop owners, disk jockeys, and individual buyers. . . . The lightness of 45, coupled with their doughnut shape and the large spindle of 45 players, also produced faster, easier listening. The "search" for the small hole in the center of the 78 was eliminated, and a listener could quickly skim through a large group of records, playing or rejecting them at a moment's notice. The process of playing records therefore became more casual, and there was a more immediate relationship between listener and record than had been possible with the heavy and breakable 78s.[4]

After television began to create a new orality, radio stations that played 45-rpm records could, and did, serve as a tribal drum by speeding up the pace and diction that the announcers used. These media changes naturally accompanied changes in singers and the songs they sang.

"It's got a good beat. You can dance to it." This cliché from the fifties sums up the crucial change that rock 'n' roll represents. In the new orality, people wanted to hear the tribal drum, not the lush

4. Carl Belz, *The Story of Rock,* p. 54.

melodies of previous popular music. "Melody, the *melos modos*, 'the road round,' is a continuous, connected, and repetitive structure that is not used in the 'cool' art of the Orient" (p. vi). Literate people disliked the new music because of the total physical involvement of dancing that the beat implied. The beat also made the words largely irrelevant, as at the beginning of Little Richard's "Tutti Frutti": "A wop bop a loo bop a lop bam boom." Actually, this extreme style continued the experiments of futurist poets with purely associative sounds. Russian poets called this style "trans-sense language." But of all the groups and performers of the fifties, from Bill Haley and the Comets to Elvis Presley, no single performer made more characteristic records than Chuck Berry.

Chuck Berry's career as a hitmaker coincided almost exactly with the period of rock 'n' roll, and his style remains essentially unchanged. He had an extraordinary capacity to create verbal icons in a universally accessible style. For example, he sensed the oral structure of the new music when he sang in "Johnny B. Goode":

> He never learned to read or write so well,/ But he could play a guitar just like ringing a bell.

Two of his best songs, "Roll Over, Beethoven," and "Brown-Eyed Handsome Man," articulate a reaction against literacy. Great tension still existed between popular and high culture (and hence gave rise to many comedy routines on television), and "Roll Over, Beethoven," which singles out music's great individualist, asserts the power of the new rhythmic music. A joke about the Venus de Milo in "Brown-Eyed Handsome Man" expresses the same tension, and even has a precedent in modernism. Berry's witticism gives a verbal equivalent to Duchamp's mustachioed Mona Lisa, "L.H.O.O.Q." The two men were using different means to express a common distaste for the high-definition, representational art of classical antiquity and the Renaissance.[5] In "Maybelline," Berry created a three-minute Populist epic, in which the hero-narrator, who drives a Ford, the car of the common man, catches Maybelline, who has gone for a ride in his rival's Cadillac.

Television turned high school, the primary institution for inculcating literacy, into an art form. Although the film *Blackboard Jungle* first

5. Cf. Bob Dylan's subsequent comment on the demise of perspective in painting in "Visions of Johanna."

made this apparent, no one wrote better high school songs than Chuck Berry, with "School Days," "Sweet Little Sixteen," and "Anthony Boy." The great popularity of high school songs, and or pseudo-religious songs—such as "Teen Angel" and "My Prayer"—and Chuck Berry's patriotic "Back in the U.S.A." illustrate the manner in which the content of each medium is another medium. Before television, the experience of high school, the sentimentality of American religion, and patriotism, were everyone's water. After television, they became art forms.

The great significance of high school songs and their rapid disappearance (the Beach Boys' early hit "Be True to Your School" was probably the last one) demonstrates the manner in which media process the changes in institutional relationships. Teenagers continued to go to proms, and get excited about Friday night football games, of course, but they did so with the sense of participation in the larger society that made more high school songs unnecessary. (The song "High School U.S.A."—and the Beach Boys' variant "Surfin' U.S.A." —made the connection between the individual place, and the nation as a whole, in a very direct way.)

Television began to make people aware of their interrelationships, and in May 1954—just after the number of television sets in America surpassed that of radios—the Supreme Court found that separate schools for blacks and whites could not also be equal. Thus began a tension between fragmentation and implosion in American politics which, to some extent, ended with the resignation of President Nixon. However, it took three years for the tension between the centralizing power of the federal government and the supposedly autonomous power of the states to reach a breaking point.

In 1957, President Eisenhower created the Civil Rights Division, which played a crucial role in the social change of the sixties, and integrated Central High School, in Little Rock, Arkansas, by sending federal troops to that tense city. In doing so, Eisenhower was enforcing centralization by breaking down local autonomy, which the representatives of linear tribalism had hardened into a dogma for its own sake. Essentially, the civil rights movement meant centralization as long as it lasted in its classical form. But soon after the passage of the civil rights bill in 1964, many of the attitudes that had seemed so pure and good began to smack of paternalism, i.e., literacy. Militant black groups who wanted autonomy, not centralization, began to appear. This meant that a new medium had changed the now familiar, com-

fortable relationships of the fifties. For the young, anyhow, that medium was stereophonic sound, which Columbia Records first mar-
keted in 1958.

Stereo meant a change from the 45-rpm record to the long-
playing album, and the media complex of the fifties. Mick Jagger
sensed this when he sneered at that complex in "Satisfaction":

> When I'm driving in my car,/ And a man comes on the radio/
> Telling me more and more/ 'Bout some useless information/
> Supposed to defy my imagination. . . .

People began to perceive the car radio, the tribal drum of the fifties,
as part of the literate, commercial culture they wished to reject. The
very music of the fifties, with its tight stanzas, neat rhymes, and
uniform beat began to seem as dull as a crew cut. By 1968 Frank
Zappa, the Marcel Duchamp of rock, could say, "It is laughable now
to think of that dull thud on the second and fourth [beat] as lewd and
pulsating."[6] Yet by 1968, people like Zappa had forgotten the contro-
versy that attended the birth of rock 'n' roll.

Although this chapter deals mainly with music, two problems of
the late sixties, university riots and the use of drugs are so important
and so much a part of rock that they deserve a few comments. If high
school appeared as an art form in the fifties, it also seemed permanent
and inevitable. Juvenile delinquents (to use a phrase of the time),
turned to violence mostly out of despair, as in *Blackboard Jungle* and
Rebel Without a Cause. In the sixties, people saw that popular action
could bring about some change, however partial and gradual. This
knowledge made the nihilism of the fifties passé, and attempts to
change, not destroy, the literate, highly centralized university structure
followed. Given the intensity of the times, violence ensued, as at
Columbia University in the spring of 1968.

Speaking of violence, the war in Vietnam has the same kind of
meaning for postmodernism that World War I had for modernism.
Both wars evoked protest (artistic and political) and interest in pa-
cifism, and generated a cultural malaise, a sense of the loss of innocence, which found expression in a spate of brilliant art works in the
years following their uneasy termination.

In the middle and late sixties, many musicians and others began
taking LSD, yet no one seems to have noticed that they were actually

6. Frank Zappa, "The Oracle Has It All Psyched Out," p. 86.

taking advantage of its therapeutic value. (That drugs subsequently became an end in themselves does not alter the validity of this statement.) Bernard Rimland's *Infantile Autism* makes it possible to integrate the use of LSD, current neurological theory, and McLuhan's theory of media. As we know, the lack of awareness of others, the obsessively literal thought, and inability to comprehend wholes, which characterize the autistic child, represent extreme forms of literate or linear thought. Rimland opposed autism to schizophrenia, which we can interpret here as an extreme form of oral, nonlinear thought.

> Differences in the symptomatology of early infantile autism and schizophrenia appear to reflect differences in the manner in which stimuli are associated with memory. Our hypothesis is that in autism necessary neural connections are made with extreme difficulty and only the strongest and most relevant impulses traverse the pathways, while in schizophrenia associations are made *too* freely, sometimes almost randomly. Stated differently, in autism it seems that the mental associations made by the afflicted child are exceedingly limited, that he has access only to highly specific fragments of memory. The schizophrenic child, in contrast, appears to be pathologically *unrestrained by relevance in making associations.*[7]

Now if the creative musicians of the sixties began to feel their literacy as undesirable, this meant that they sensed their inability to make associations. People like Ken Kesey, who began using LSD very early, knew of its therapeutic value in helping to make these associations. To cite Rimland again:

> LSD-25, which produces schizophrenia-like symptoms in normal persons, exerts an *excitant* effect on the reticular formation and a heightened awareness of sensory stimuli. . . . LSD may prove useful in facilitating reticular formation. In other words, LSD or a similar drug may have a normalizing effect on autistic children.[8]

In the sixties, "mind" came to mean "literacy"; "blowing your mind" meant using LSD to blow open channels of association that literacy had closed. (A "heavy metal" group from Detroit, the MC5, called their theme song "Kick Out the Jams.")

---

7. Bernard Rimland, *Infantile Autism: The Syndrome and Its Implications for a Neural Theory of Behavior,* p. 165. Rimland's emphasis.

8. Ibid., p. 169.

Acid trips affected many forms of expression in the sixties, of course, but not quite in the way that most people have assumed. People usually think that the musicians took acid, and then wrote down what they saw and/or experienced. But this attitude, like so many other interpretations of popular culture, simply continues the premises of nineteenth-century realism, which state that the artist reproduces that which is "out there" in some sense. (The shift from an external to an internal landscape in no way implies a change in paradigm.) One can interpret acid-inspired rock as an interaction of tradition and cultural process by saying that acid made people more sensitive to European surrealism and decadence and that the artists could therefore draw on this tradition, which had become acceptable —i.e., no longer perceived as belonging to high culture—to their listeners. Dylan's perceptions in his music, for instance, have definite affinities with surrealism (see the liner notes to his album *Desire* for a highly significant reference to Rimbaud), as did Jim Morrison, who knew modern poetry well. Surrealism created some biographical precedents for the artists, also.

In several ways, the best example one can cite is Alfred Jarry, who found his *lycée,* and especially the man who taught Newtonian physics, intensely alienating. The physics teacher became a crucial figure in his principal work, the play *Ubu Roi* (1896). Jarry tried to liberate himself from his literacy through alcohol and eventually drank himself to death—more or less deliberately. Brian Epstein, Brian Jones, Jimi Hendrix, and Janis Joplin did much the same thing, with the difference that they combined alcohol and drugs. Jim Morrison, lead singer and songwriter for the strongly expressionist group The Doors, resembled Jarry not merely in that both were alcoholics; both burnt themselves out at an early age in an attempt to alter the distinctions between life and theater. Jarry and Morrison both died primarily because they had no desire to live any longer.

And Elvis had no desire to live any longer, either. When one of the greatest performers in American history dies a nonviolent death at the age of forty-two, it is such an extraordinary event that I wish to insert a few comments on it here. One can say that Elvis died because he couldn't think of anything to do except drive one of his Stutz Bearcats around Memphis at night. That is to say, he had an instructively American kind of greatness.

When people write about Elvis, they often begin by commenting on a haunting photograph of Elvis and his parents that someone took in 1937, when Elvis was two years old. Greil Marcus, in his brilliant —really incomparable—book *Mystery Train: Images of America in Rock 'n' Roll Music,* calls the faces of Elvis's parents "vacant," and they are that. But they also have a familiar quality. We know them well, because we have seen their likes before. James Agee and Walker Evans spent most of the summer of 1936 in northern Alabama, less than a hundred miles from Tupelo, doing the fieldwork for what became *Let Us Now Praise Famous Men.* And Evans, in now-famous photographs recorded just the painful, hopeless faces that Elvis's parents have. Their faces have little in common with those of the folks who live in those big white houses with tall columns which figure so prominently in Southern myths. In the Delta, where those houses do exist, the well-to-do whites drank mint juleps and become social climbers. Significantly, the Mississippi Delta has produced many great black artists—like Robert Johnson—but no great white artists.

Elvis's Mississippi, Tupelo, a trading center for the rural areas of the northeast part of the state, had little in common with the Delta, even though the Delta was only about eighty miles away. For Tupelo is located in the hill country, and it was simply not profitable to own slaves there. In fact, Winston County, Alabama, where Agee and Evans spent some of their time, actually seceded from the Confederacy; the hill people there decided that this was a rich folks' war, and that the rich folks could fight it themselves. Thus it happened that the hill country of the South became, and stayed, poor, protestant, and puritan. As such, it produced the vacant faces of Elvis's parents, and the shapeless clothing they wear. One looks in vain for a relationship between the adults' sadness (they look defeated as only poor Southerners can look, and Evans taught us to see their dignity in this defeat), and the boy's smile. This tension between the parents and the child really means a tension between the inadequacy of Tupelo as an environment and the boy's still undeveloped talent. Elvis lived in Tupelo for thirteen years, and I suggest that during those thirteen years that tension created his indomitable ambition, which we never understood before Marcus's book. The pain and hurt of being a poor Southern boy in those bare hills gave power to the jaunty, yet visceral assertiveness that made Elvis a censored sensation on the Ed Sullivan Show eighteen years after the photograph was taken.

I sensed something of the pent-up drive the only time I saw Elvis perform in person. He came back to Tupelo in October of 1956 to do two shows after he had finished making *Love Me Tender.* (Rumor had it that Natalie Wood had made the shirts he wore.) But, mostly, I remember the National Guard. The day Elvis came to town, there was a National Guardsman standing on every street corner downtown, and each one held a rifle with a fixed bayonet. I had never seen soldiers hold rifles like that before, and they seemed disturbing; I didn't know it then, but they anticipated the soldiers who would integrate Central High School in Little Rock the next fall. For the agitation Elvis evoked manifested the same energy of social change as that of the other upheavals in the South that coincided with his career.

The very orality that Elvis embodied was being fragmented by the process whose energy made him famous; as the rest of the country became more oral, the South became more literate. During his campaign, Jimmy Carter accurately commented that he could never have become a candidate for president if it had not been for Martin Luther King. King's work gave great impetus to the fragmentation of local power structures in the South. The fragmentation of those power structures necessarily preceded the merger of Southern politics into national politics. (Incidentally, King used the rhythms of Southern protestantism for political purposes as Elvis used them for artistic purposes. Somehow, Southern protestantism becomes communicable outside the South only in nonreligious forms.)

Elvis changed the way people dressed and sang and felt about their bodies, and he could do so because of the extraordinary openness and permeability that literacy has produced in American society. That openness means that American society can absorb and commercialize anything—and it absorbed and commercialized Elvis. Once Elvis had gotten out of Tupelo—metaphorically speaking—and had become rich and famous as few people have ever been, he became great and irrelevant in equal measure. Elvis agreed to become a product, and products do not confront pain and despair. His movies expressed the mindless optimism which his life, and voice, and body, negated at every instant.

Elvis's first big record for Sun, "That's All Right," expressed the anger and hostility between the sexes that intense change evokes, and "Heartbreak Hotel" gave a surrealistic image of our loneliness in a fragmented society. Although Elvis believed in what he was, he never believed in what he could do, and never wanted to find out. Thus, his later records never took chances, and he had to rely on other people's words in an age when performers wrote their own songs. And when he performed, he never chose songs which resonate within the heart of darkness at the center of the American dream, such as Bruce Springsteen's "Born to Run." As a result, in his last years he resembled a dynamo that generated great power but couldn't transmit it. His body became blocked—it eloquently expressed the way his greatness was blocked—and the energy turned in on him, and killed him.

The house in which Elvis was born is now a monument, of course, and forms part of Elvis Presley Park in East Tupelo, that part of town which was always on the other side of the tracks. I don't suppose that the people of Tupelo meant it this way, but Elvis's birthplace stands near the intersection of Presley and Berry Streets. The unconscious reference to the greatest performer of the fifties and the greatest songwriter of the fifties stands there unnoticed, as a suggestion of the South's role in unifying American music.

But a unity seeks to enlarge itself, and the new electric environment of the sixties made people want to learn from other parts of the world, and when the Beatles and the Beach Boys went to India to meditate, reporters found this startling and newsworthy. Because of the ever-present distinction between art and entertainment, no one stopped to think that these performers went to India for reasons similar to those which caused Rilke to go to Russia, and caused Gide and Klee to go to Tunisia. In fact, in visiting the East and taking an interest in nonlinear thought patterns, the musicians were doing what a large number of other European artists had done, because rock music continued the same process that began with modernism.

The Beatles began this, of course, with *Sergeant Pepper's Lonely Hearts Club Band,* but they recorded their masterpiece in 1968: *The Beatles.* This album uses as an art form the 45-rpm record that the Beatles first encountered as an American product with the work of American artists like Chuck Berry and Elvis Presley. As one listens to this album again and again, one realizes that the United States itself, as the most literate country in the world, becomes an art form. Of this great album, I can only discuss the first song, "Back in the U.S.S.R.," because of the way it uses the 45-rpm record.

"Back in the U.S.S.R." begins with a demonstration of the stereo effect when a jet plane passes from left to right. This emphasizes the difference between the album's style and that of the monophonic 45. The Beatles recall the fifties with the standard rock 'n' roll complement of guitars and drums, and closely paraphrase Chuck Berry's "Back in the U.S.A." of course, but with the crucial difference that by the pun on the U.S./U.S.S.R. they convey the similarity of tribal linearity and linear tribalism. They beautifully express these similarities when they adopt the Beach Boys' falsetto style. Moreover, the second verse specifically refers to Brian Wilson's classic "California Girls"; Lennon–McCartney wittily substitute the Ukraine, in southern Russia, for southern California. The Beach Boys appear here because, more than that of any group before the rise of acid rock, the Beach Boys' music represented a way of life—the American devotion to life, liberty, and the pursuit of happiness. By combining innocent hedonism with complex counterpoint, the Beach Boys expressed the American myth as very few artists in our society ever have, and the fact that no individual member of the group has become a star in his own right merely emphasizes the cohesive force of that myth.

If the content of the 45-rpm record seemed foreign, its use of the recurring beat did not, because it structured a nonlinear use of language and experience. In "My Back Pages," Dylan explains that literacy (note the irony of the title) caused a dissociation of sensibility within his psyche in the past; but the chorus expresses the irrelevance of chronological, Newtonian time. In a wonderful play on words, Dylan states that implosion has brought with it a resurgence of the libido, in the Jungian sense, and thus of youth.

Rock also used some explicitly mythical concepts of the eternal return of existence, as in "Turn! Turn! Turn!" by the Byrds, whose words Pete Seeger adapted from Ecclesiastes. A little later Joni Mitchell used the image of the carousel for an explicit statement of the eternal return in "The Circle Game":

And the seasons they go round and round/ And the painted ponies go up and down/ We're captive on the carousel of time/ We can't return we can only look/ Behind from where we came/ And go round and round and round in the circle game./

Since print can convey none of the textual qualities of rock—the tape effects, multiple dubbing, key changes, and all the rest, it seems simplest to conclude this discussion of rock with some remarks about the songwriter whose work suffers least when abstracted from the sound of the record, Bob Dylan.[9] A comment from Ong's *The Pres-*

9. Cf. Dave Van Ronk's testimony that Dylan owed a conscious debt to modernism: "When he [Dylan] had a place of his own, I went up there and on the bookshelf was a volume of French poets from Nerval to almost the present. I think it ended at Apollinaire, and it included Rimbaud, and it was all

ence of the Word gives a leading idea: "Since sound is indicative of here-and-now activity, the word as sound establishes here-and-now presence."[10] The spoken word, by its very nature, implies the presence of another who can hear it. The spoken word creates a conversation, a binary whole. The particular power of Dylan's songs comes from his ability to restore this binary quality to the word. To be sure, poets have addressed ballads to the beloved from time immemorial, but before Dylan literacy had made the address meaningless, and rendered it a lifeless convention, like the unity of time in eighteenth-century neoclassical drama. A hit of the early fifties, "Let Me Go, Lover," provides a good example of the convention for its own sake. Two aspects of Dylan's records make the difference: his obviously untrained, rasping (Riegl would have called it "tactile") voice that drew on the "talking blues" tradition, and his ability, reminiscent of Pound's, to use colloquial English for startling imagistic effects. When Dylan addresses a "you," he demands a reply, as in the famous refrain of "Ballad of a Thin Man."

A great many of Dylan's songs simply continue the tradition of ballad address in a fresher, more vivid style. Whatever their differences, "Boots of Spanish Leather," "Honey, Just Allow Me One More Chance," "It Ain't Me, Babe," and "Temporary Like Achilles" are all addressed to a girl. This strain culminates in "I'll Be Your Baby Tonight" on *John Wesley Harding,* and the mellow classics of *Nashville Skyline,* "Lay Lady Lay," "Tell Me That It Isn't True," and "Tonight I'll Be Staying Here With You." Had Dylan written only songs like these, which I call his "private" dialogue songs, he would have reinvigorated a tradition, but would not have attracted such intense feelings. His major importance comes from his two other groups of songs, his "public" dialogue songs, and his surrealist songs. The masterpieces occur as a fusion of the two groups.

In discussing Dylan's public-dialogue songs, one should keep in mind two of Eliot's statements that Dylan has always implicitly understood, and that his admirers have rarely understood: "In writing himself, the great poet writes his time," and "The emotion of art is impersonal." As a comment in the liner notes to *The Freewheelin' Bob*

---

well-thumbed with passages underlined and notes in the margins." Quoted in Anthony Scaduto, "Bob Dylan: An Intimate Biography. Part I," *Rolling Stone,* p. 39.

10. Walter J. Ong, S.J., *The Presence of the Word,* p. 113.

Dylan attests, Dylan knew that the great blues singers were not just "expressing themselves," as romantics usually believe. He knew that they were using the discipline of a tradition—just as Picasso had known that the makers of African masks were not indulging in an "aesthetic operation." Because of his consciousness of the impersonal quality of what he was doing, he could adopt the pose of the bard who voiced the feelings of the tribe to threatening outsiders. Love, past or present, appears in his private-dialogue songs; hate, or at best, distaste, appears in the public dialogue, or protest, songs such as "The Times They Are A Changin' " and "Blowin' in the Wind." Yet Dylan's supreme achievements occur when he uses this public dialogue in a surrealistic way.

One of the songs on *Highway 61 Revisited,* "Desolation Row," absolutely demands a few special comments. "Row" suggests the sequential nature of print, of course, and the phrase "Desolation Row" images print as what Eliot and Mumford called a wasteland. As usual, Dylan's images of violence in "Desolation Row" evoke associations with literacy. To put the matter far less forcefully than Dylan did, in this song the representatives of literacy want to keep people from escaping to Desolation Row because an awareness of the desolation of literacy implies a rejection of it.

The sixties ended quite abruptly, on the afternoon of 6 December 1969, at the Rolling Stones' free concert at Altamont, California, when the Hell's Angels stomped a black man to death while Mick Jagger was singing "Under My Thumb." The chaos of that afternoon eventually forced people to confront the inadequacies of their belief in flower power and the love generation. After Altamont, the sixties seemed literate, and hence naive, just as the seventies eventually will. The energy of implosion then became more diffuse, and the Beatles ceased to function as a whole that was greater than the sum of its parts. When the energy of the process no longer operated through them, the Beatles, and the members of the other groups that broke up, simply became talented professional musicians. John Lennon even said in an interview about a year after Altamont:

> The dream is over. It's just the same, only I'm thirty, and a lot of people have got long hair. That's what it is, man, nothing happened except that we grew up, we did our thing—just like they were telling us.[11]

11. Quoted in *Rolling Stone,* 4 February 1971, p. 37.

All the creative movements of the twentieth century have had a self-liquidating quality. Their ability to bring about revolutions in sensibility presupposes a certain tension between the artist and the public. As the work communicates between the artist and the public, it eases this tension, and thus liquidates its own rationale.

Don McLean's "American Pie" became the most important song of the early seventies precisely because it turned the fifties and sixties into an art form. (The movie *American Graffiti* and the television show "Happy Days" have had an analogous function, yet neither has elicited a musical response as intense as "Killing Me Softly," Roberta Flack's response to "American Pie.") "American Pie" has one characteristic feature of the poetry of traditional oral societies—formulas. The formulas of "American Pie" come from the only viable cultural tradition that America can have—a tradition of artifacts and images that have found widespread acceptance.

"American Pie" really amounts to a formulaic history of the period 1955–1970; its references range from Marty Robbins and a fifties hit by the Monotones called "The Book of Love" to Altamont. The song, with its nonlinear syntax, would simply make no sense to anyone who did not know rock 'n' roll—and rock. While Eliot and other modernists used formulas, they proceeded rather differently. By incorporating the whole of world literature as a "simultaneous order" of formulas, they made demands on their audience that necessarily limited it. Whatever their other problems, songwriters of today do not have this one, for they can validly assume that records, radio, and concerts have made the music of the fifties and sixties part of the consciousness of the audience. (In addition to "American Pie," hear also Rick Nelson's "Garden Party," with its references to Chuck Berry, and Elton John's "Crocodile Rock," which uses the melody of Paul Anka's "Diana" in the chorus.)

This use of formulas, which constantly recurs in the brilliant prose of *Rolling Stone* as well, expresses a shared, tribal consciousness we didn't have before The Beatles. For all the cultural significance of formulas, however, we find it difficult to institutionalize them, and as a result lyrics have played a relatively insignificant role in the work of the four most creative groups of the early seventies: the Allman Brothers and Santana from the United States, and Pink Floyd and Yes from Great Britain.

The phenomenal success of the film *Love Story* signaled to many people a "Return to Romance," as *Time* called its cover story on Ali

McGraw. Actually, *Love Story* may have defined the most general process of the seventies: a synthesis of literacy and the new orality. A culture can change only so rapidly, and after the period of intense implosion in the sixties, literate structures such as love stories seem comforting to many. (Hear the hit by Paul McCartney and Wings, "Silly Love Songs.") An analysis of country and western music, which has replaced rock as the most meaningful American idiom,[12] might well elicit this ambivalence. Country and western music has generally expressed fragmentation by turning rural life into an art form, but television has recently cooled it off.

Someone has said, "Times which are interesting to read about are not pleasant to live through." Certainly, we cannot expect tranquillity as a characteristic of implosion, and this fact has created great problems for popular culture, which usually accedes to its audience's demand for affirmation—for obsessive cheerfulness and the happy ending—above all. In the sixties, popular music at its best offered catharsis, not overt affirmation, and thus achieved extraordinary power and meaning. But catharsis can occur only after a genuine confrontation with pain, and in the more diffuse situation that came into being in the late sixties, we cannot assume that we can achieve catharsis through media experiences that we can all share. It may help to keep in mind these lines from John Fogerty's "Bad Moon Rising":

> Hope you've got your things together/ Hope that you are quite prepared to die/ Looks like we in for nasty weather/ One eye is taken for an eye./

12. The polyphonically structured film *Nashville* makes this apparent. As Robert Altman has said, the film is not about Nashville, but about America. (I suggest that insofar as the film is "about" anything, it is "about" power: what people will do to get it, and what it does to them after they get it.) Rock musicians could not now present sufficiently general meaning for the current stage of America's process.

Bibliography

Allport, Floyd H. *Theories of Perception and the Concept of Structure*. New York: John Wiley, 1955.

Arp, Hans (Jean). *On My Way: Poetry and Essays, 1912–1947*. New York: Wittenborn, Schultz, 1948.

Barthélemy-Jodaule, Madeleine. *Bergson et Teilhard de Chardin*. Paris: Editions de Seuil, 1963.

Barthes, Roland. *Systeme de la Mode*. Paris: Editions de Seuil, 1967.

Baumgart, Fritz. *A History of Architectural Styles*. New York: Praeger, 1971.

Belinsky, V. G. *Sobranie sochinenii*. 3 vols. Edited by F. M. Golovenchenko. Moscow, 1948.

Bell, Clive. *Art*. New York: Capricorn Books, 1958.

Belz, Carl. *The Story of Rock*. New York: Oxford University Press, 1969.

Berger, Peter L., and Luckmann, Thomas. *The Social Construction of Reality*. Garden City: Doubleday Anchor Books, 1967.

Bergson, Henri. *Oeuvres*. Paris: Presses Universitaires de France, 1959.

Bloch, Walter. *Politaritat*. Berlin: Duncker und Humbolt, 1972.

Burnham, Jack. *Beyond Modern Sculpture*. New York: G. Braziller, 1968.

Čapek, Milič. *Bergson and Modern Physics: A Reinterpretation and Re-Evaluation*. Boston Studies in the Philosophy of Science, VIII. Dordrecht: D. Reidel, 1971.

_____. *The Philosophical Impact of Contemporary Physics*. Princeton: Van Nostrand, 1961.

Carnap, Rudolph. *Philosophical Foundations of Physics*. Edited by Martin Gardner. New York: Basic Books, 1966.

Cassirer, Ernst. *The Philosophy of Symbolic Forms*. 3 vols. New Haven: Yale University Press, 1953–1957.

Chardin, Pierre Teilhard de. *L'Activation de l'Énergie*. Paris: Editions de Seuil, 1963.

_____. *L'Avenir de l'Homme*. Paris: Editions de Seuil. 1959.

_____. *The Phenomenon of Man*. Translated by Bernard Wall. Introduction by Julian Huxler. Rev. ed. New York: Harper and Row, 1959.

Cherniavsky, Michael. *Tsar and People.* New Haven: Yale University Press, 1961.

Chomsky, Noam. *Current Issues in Linguistic Theory.* The Hague: Mouton, 1966.

Curran, Michael. "Vladimir Stasov and the Development of Russian National Art, 1851–1910." Ph.D. dissertation, University of Michigan, 1965.

Curtis, James M. "Marshall McLuhan and French Structuralism." *Boundary 2* 1:1 (Fall 1972): 134–36.

DeLong, Howard. *A Profile of Mathematical Logic.* Reading, Mass.: Addison-Wesley, 1970.

Dennis, George. "Education," in *McGraw-Hill Encyclopedia of Russia and the Soviet Union.* Edited by Michael T. Florinsky. New York: McGraw-Hill, 1961.

Derrida, Jacques. "White Mythology: Metaphor in the Text of Philosophy." *New Literary History* 61:1 (Autumn 1974): 5–74.

Dessauer, Friedrich. *Streit um die Technik.* Frankfurt am Main: J. Knecht, 1956.

Deutscher, Isaac. *Stalin: A Political Biography.* New York and London: Oxford University Press, 1949.

Diedrich, Otto. *Hitler.* Translated by Richard Winston and Clara Winston. Chicago: Henry Regnery, 1955.

Donato, Eugenio. "The Two Languages of Criticism," in *The Languages of Criticism and the Sciences of Man,* pp. 89–97. Edited by Richard Macksey and Eugenio Donato. Baltimore and London: The Johns Hopkins Press, 1970.

Duffy, Dennis. *Marshall McLuhan.* Toronto-Montreal: McClelland and Steward Limited, 1969.

Eager, Gerald. "The Missing and the Mutilated Eye in Contemporary Art." *Journal of Aesthetics and Art Criticism* 20 (Fall 1961): 49–60.

Eddington, Arthur. *The Nature of the Physical World.* New York: Macmillan, 1929.

Einstein, Albert. *The Meaning of Relativity.* 5th ed. Princeton: Princeton University Press, 1955.

Eliot, T. S. *Selected Essays.* New York: Harcourt Brace, 1932.

———. "Review of *The Path of the Rainbow: An Anthology of Songs and Chants from the Indians of North America,* ed. George W. Cronyn." *Atheneum* (17 October 1919): 1036.

Ellul, Jacques. *The Technological Society.* New York: Alfred A. Knopf, 1964.

Faulkner, William. *The Portable Faulkner.* Edited by Malcolm Cowley. New York: Viking Press, 1951.

_____. *The Sound and the Fury.* New York: Modern Library, 1946.

Fermi, Laura. *Mussolini.* Chicago: University of Chicago Press, 1961.

Fiedler, Leslie. "Cross the Border, Close the Gap," in *The Collected Essays of Leslie Fiedler,* 2:461–85. New York: Stein and Day, 1977.

Fisher, J. L. "Art Styles as Cultural Cognitive Maps." *American Anthropologist* 63 (1961): 79–93.

Fitzgerald, F. Scott. *The Great Gatsby.* New York: Charles Scribner's Sons, 1953.

Frank, Phillip. *Einstein, His Life and Times.* Translated by George Rosen. Edited by Shuichi Kusaka. New York: Alfred A. Knopf, 1947.

Gebser, Jean. *Ursprung und Gegenwart.* 2 vols. Stuttgart: Deutsche Verlag-Anstalt, 1949–1953.

Gilot, Françoise. *Life with Picasso.* New York: McGraw-Hill, 1964.

Goldmann, Lucien. *The Hidden God.* Translated by Phillip Thody. New York: The Humanities Press, 1964.

Graves, John. *The Conceptual Foundations of Contemporary Relativity Theory.* Cambridge: The MIT Press, 1971.

Gregor, A. James. *The Ideology of Fascism.* New York: The Free Press, 1969.

Grohmann, Will. *Wassily Kandinsky.* New York: Harry N. Abrams, n.d.

Grünbaum, Adolph. *Modern Science and Zeno's Paradoxes.* Middletown, Conn.: Wesleyan University Press, 1967.

Harris, Marvin. *The Rise of Anthropological Theory.* New York: Thomas Y. Crowell, 1968.

Harris, Thomas B. *I'm OK—You're OK: A Practical Guide to Transactional Analysis.* New York and Evanston: Harper and Row, 1969.

Hegel, Georg Wilhelm Friedrich. *Sämtliche Werke.* 22 vols. Edited by Hermann Glockner. Stuttgart: F. Fromanns Verlag, 1958.

Holroyd, Michael. *Lytton Strachey.* 2 vols. London: William Heineman, 1968.

Hughes, H. Stuart. *Consciousness and Society.* New York: Vintage Books, 1958.

Hulme, T. E. *Speculations.* Edited by Herbert Read. London: Kegan Paul, 1924.

Infeld, Leopold. *Albert Einstein, His Work and Its Influence on Our World.* New York: Charles Scribner's Sons, 1950.

Jones, Alun. *The Life and Opinions of T. E. Hulme.* Boston: Beacon Press, 1960.

Jung, Carl G. *Collected Works: Symbols of Transformation.* Vol 5. New York: Pantheon Books, 1956.

Kapp, Ernst. *Grundlinien einer Philosophie der Technik.* Braunschweig: George Westermann, 1877.

―――. *Vergleichende allgemeine Erdkunde in wissenschaftlicher Darstellung.* 2d ed. rev. Braunschweig: George Westermann, 1868.

Karbusicky, Vladimir. *Wiederspiegelungstheorie und Strukturalismus.* Munich: Wilhelm Fink Verlag, 1973.

Khruschev, Nikita. *Khrushchev Remembers.* Edited by Edward Crankshaw. Boston: Little, Brown, 1970.

Klee, Paul. *The Diaries of Paul Klee.* Edited by Felix Klee. Berkeley: University of California Press, 1968.

Körner, Stephen. "On the Relevance of Post-Godelian Mathematics to Philosophy," in *Problems in the Philosophy of Mathematics,* pp. 118–32. Edited by Imre Lakatos. Amsterdam: North-Holland Publishing Company, 1967.

Kuhn, Thomas S. *The Structure of Scientific Revolutions.* 2d ed. Chicago: University of Chicago Press, 1970.

Lakatos, Imre. "Falsification and the Methodology of Scientific Research Programmes," in *Criticism and the Growth of Knowledge,* pp. 91–146. Edited by Imre Lakatos and Alan Musgrave. Cambridge: Cambridge University Press, 1970.

Lange, John. *Binary.* New York: Alfred A. Knopf, 1972.

Lehmann-Haupt, Helmut. *Art Under a Dictatorship.* New York: Oxford University Press, 1954.

Lenin, V. I. *Polnoe sobranie sochinenii.* 5th ed. 40 vols. Moscow, 1961.

Lennon, John. "The Rolling Stone Interview: John Lennon." *Rolling Stone* (4 February 1971): 36–43.

Lerner, Daniel. *The Passing of Traditional Society.* New York: The Free Press, 1964.

Levi-Strauss, Claude. *The Raw and the Cooked.* New York: Harper and Row, 1969.

Lewis, Wyndham. *Time and Western Man.* Boston: Beacon Press, 1957.

Lotman, Yury. *Struktura khudozhestvennogo teksta.* Moscow: "Iskusstvo," 1970.

Lucas, J. R. "Minds, Machines, and Gödel." *Philosophy* 36 (1961): 112–27.

McLuhan, Marshall. *Understanding Media.* New York: McGraw-Hill, 1964.

McLuhan, Marshall, and Fiore, Quentin. *War and Peace in the Global Village.* New York: Bantam Books, 1968.

Mandelstam, Osip. *Sobranie sochinenii.* 3 vols. Edited by Gleb Struve and Boris Fillipov. Washington, D. C.: Inter-Language Associates, 1966.

Marcus, Greil. *Mystery Train: Images of America in Rock 'n' Roll Music.* New York: E. P. Dutton, 1976.

Mercier, André. "Knowledge and Physical Reality," in *Physics, Logic and History,* pp. 39–58. Edited by Wolfgang Yourgrau and Allen B. Breck. New York: Plenum Press, 1970.

Miller, Geoffrey. "The Story of P." *Harper's* (October 1974): 6–12.

Morris, Lloyd. *Not So Long Ago.* New York: Random House, 1949.

Müller-Markus, S. "Einstein and Soviet Philosophy." *Studies in Soviet Thought* 1 (1961): 78–87.

Mumford, Lewis. *The City in History.* New York: Harcourt, Brace, and World, 1961.

_____. *Sticks and Stones: A Study of American Architecture and Civilization.* New York: Boni and Liveright, 1924.

_____. *Technics and Civilization.* New York: Harcourt, Brace, and World, 1963.

Nevins, Allan, and Hill, Frank Ernest. *Ford. II: Expansion and Challenge, 1915–1933.* New York: Charles Scribner's Sons, 1957.

Nicolson, Marjorie Hope. *Newton Demands the Muse.* Princeton: Princeton University Press, 1946.

_____. *The Breaking of the Circle.* Rev. ed. New York: Columbia University Press, 1960.

Nietzsche, Friedrich. *Sämtliche Werke.* 12 vols. Stuttgart: Alfred Kroner Verlag, 1952–1959.

Novalis (Friedrich von Hardenberg). *Schriften.* 4 vols. Edited by Paul Kluckhohn and Richard Samuel. Stuttgart: W. Kohlhammer Verlag, 1960–1975.

Odum, Eugene P., with Odum, Howard T. *Fundamentals of Ecology.* Philadelphia: W. D. Sanders, 1959.

Ong, Walter J., S. J. *The Presence of the Word.* New Haven: Yale University Press, 1967.

_____. "World as View and World as Event." *American Anthropologist* 71:4 (August 1969): 634–47.

Peips, Leida. Letter to L. I. Brezhnev. *Pravda* (5 February 1975), p. 1.

Perls, Frederick. *Gestalt Therapy Verbatim.* Edited by John O. Stevens. Lafayette, Calif.: Real People Press, 1969.

Peyre, Henri. *Les générations littéraires.* Paris: Voivin, 1948.

Piaget, Jean. *Le Structuralisme.* Paris: Presses Universitaires de France, 1970.

Pound, Ezra. *Literary Essays of Ezra Pound.* Edited by T. S. Eliot. New York: New Directions, 1968.

Progress of Literacy in Various Countries. Paris: UNESCO, 1953.

Quine, Willard Van Orman. *Ontological Relativity and Other Essays.* New York: Columbia University Press, 1969.

Riegl, Alois. *Stilfragen.* 2d ed. Berlin: Richard Carl Schmidt, 1923.

Rimland, Bernard. *Infantile Autism: The Syndrome and Its Implications for a Neural Theory of Behavior.* New York: Appleton-Century-Crofts, 1964.

Rubin, William S. *Dada, Surrealism and Their Heritage.* New York: Museum of Modern Art, 1968.

Scaduto, Anthony. "Bob Dylan: An Intimate Biography. Part I." *Rolling Stone* (2 March 1972): 36–44.

Segall, Marshall H., et al. *The Influence of Culture on Visual Perception.* Indianapolis: Bobbs-Merrill, 1966.

Sharlin, Harold I. *The Making of the Electric Age.* London: Abelard-Schuman, 1963.

Shirer, William L. *The Rise and Fall of the Third Reich.* New York: Simon and Schuster, 1961.

Solzhenitsyn, Aleksandr. *Arkhipelag Gulag.* Paris: YMCA Press, 1973.

———. *V kruge pervom.* New York and Evanston: Harper Colophon Books, 1968.

Speer, Albert. *Inside the Third Reich.* Translated by Richard Winston and Clara Winston. New York: Macmillan, 1971.

Steiner, George. *Language and Silence.* New York: Atheneum, 1967.

Stearn, Gerald Emanuel, ed. *McLuhan: Hot and Cool.* New York: Signet Books, 1967.

Theall, Donald F. *The Medium Is the Rear View Mirror.* Montreal and London: McGill-Queen's University Press, 1971.

Venturi, Robert. *Complexity and Contradiction in Modern Architecture.* New York: Museum of Modern Art, 1969.

Warshow, Robert. "The Gangster as Tragic Hero," in *The Immediate Experience.* Introduction by Lionel Trilling. Garden City: Doubleday, 1962.

Washton, Rose-Carol. "Wassily Kandinsky: Painting and Theory, 1908–1913," Ph.D. dissertation, Yale University, 1968.

Watkins, J. W. N. "Against 'Normal Science,' " in *Criticism and the Growth of Knowledge,* pp. 25–38. Edited by Imre Lakatos and Alan Musgrave. Cambridge: Cambridge University Press, 1970.

Watt, Ian. *The Rise of the Novel.* Berkeley and Los Angeles: University of California Press, 1965.

Webb, Judson. "Metamathematics and the Philosophy of Mind." *Philosophy of Science* 35 (1968): 156–78.

Wellek, René. *A History of Modern Criticism: 1750–1950. II. The Romantic Age.* New Haven: Yale University Press, 1955.

Worringer, Wilhelm. *Abstraction und Einfühlung.* Munich: R. Piper, 1959.

Young, J. Z. *Doubt and Certainty in Science.* Oxford: Clarendon Press, 1951.

Zappa, Frank. "The Oracle Has It all Psyched Out." *Life* (28 June 1968): 82–90.

Index

193